The

TRAGIC
ROMANCE
of
AFRICA

The
TRAGIC
ROMANCE
of
AFRICA

DENNIS HUBBARD
and
JONATHAN NICHOLAS

Matador
9 Priory Business Park
Kibworth Beauchamp
Leicestershire LE8 0RX, UK
Tel: (+44) 116 279 2299
Fax: (+44) 116 279 2277
Email: books@troubador.co.uk
Web: www.troubador.co.uk/matador

ISBN 978 1783061 624

British Library Cataloguing in Publication Data.
A catalogue record for this book is available from the British Library.

Typeset in 10.5 pt Stempel Garamond Roman by Troubador Publishing Ltd, Leicester, UK
Printed and bound in the UK by TJ International, Padstow, Cornwall

Matador is an imprint of Troubador Publishing Ltd

To Africa

This is a true story

CONTENTS

Preface   *x*

An Adventurous Youth   1
Employment   6
Manchester   10
London   13
The Capetown Castle   19
Cape Town: Into Africa   28
Arrival: Broken Hill   39
The New Job   46
The Police Reserve   52
"Mal mal!"   59
Mulungushi Dam   67
The Pool   77
The Kayak   81
The Rifles   88
The Kite   91
Sonny's Trip   105
The Congo   112
My Garden   119
Alec and Diana   125
Livingstone   136
Night Shoot   145
Tsetse   152
First Kill   159
The Piano   169
The Envelope   176
Rain   184
Diana   190
Charlotte and Alec   195
The End   199

Epilogue   206
Acknowledgements   208

I will tell myself the truth
Even if those around me
Deny it.

I will tell myself the truth
Even if a friendship's
Lost by it

I will seek the truth
Even if it tells me
Something horrible
With it

I will speak the truth
Even if I'm no longer
Invited in

At the end, the all I have
Is the truth

Charlotte Ballard

PREFACE

It seems incredible to me now, looking back as I have after so many years, that I once lived and worked in a remote part of Africa, surrounded by true wilderness. I had a bungalow, a job, a manservant, a kayak, a rifle, and an insatiable thirst for adventure. I had friendships the like of which, and the intensity of which, I have never experienced before or since. I lived an adventurer's dream under a huge African sky and the most sublime, clear moonlit nights. I saw wild animals of all types wandering freely and even shot at some of them occasionally with my rifle. I willingly and naively took part in some exciting events which exposed me to moments of extreme danger in a wonderful, once in a lifetime adventure in the vast emptiness and relentless heat of Africa.

My two year adventure was indeed the greatest and happiest of my life, but great tragedy also accompanied it, and some horrific, painful memories have remained to haunt me through the decades since. In fact, it was all so long ago now that my recollections of it for this book were at first cloudy and obscure, to the extent that those terrific years often seemed indistinct fragments of memory, delicate and beautiful, but entirely out of reach, like large and exquisite butterflies sealed in some dusty glass case. Many of these memories have had to be coaxed and forced, kicking and screaming from the darkest corners of my mind, from where, in order to preserve my sanity, they have lain deliberately hidden for over sixty years. But I have dragged them out into the daylight for all to see, and I've drawn them across these pages, often very painfully, in the last few years for you to read. Maybe you could eventually understand what happened to me and why I had to do what I did.

Now that I am in my eighties, in the process of writing

this book I am reminded that the callow, grinning youth in the tiny black and white faded photographs really is Dennis Hubbard; a young man who seems to be an entirely different person standing there in a bygone age of colonialism and ignorance, brutality and beauty, a time of naïve simplicity, in which I was playing my own small part in the slow, painful demise of an era that is now as far distant as my own memory.

But it all *really did happen*, as the photographs serve to remind me, along with all the surviving scribbled notes, postcards, and letters home, all of which I've used as source material for this book. I have forced my memory to recall the events of those fateful, wonderful years and commit them to these pages. Suddenly while writing, they became as clear as if they'd only just happened, even the awful experiences which I'd deliberately pushed to the back of my mind for so many years and wished to forget. But these were all part of my time there, and are just as important as the good times. It has been a cathartic exercise for me, exhausting, traumatic, but incredibly rewarding. To finally exorcise the dark side of my time in Africa, to write of the horrors that punctuated the latter days so dramatically, and which ultimately forced my departure.

I am sure there will be occasions while reading this book when you will find yourself pausing for breath, to remind yourself that this is indeed a true story, and that these incidents really did take place. I can assure you they did. Never have I known such a wild adventure with such wonderful memories, but never, thankfully, have I experienced such tragedy and heartache as was my time spent in, what is simply, the greatest continent on earth.

Dennis Hubbard, April 2013

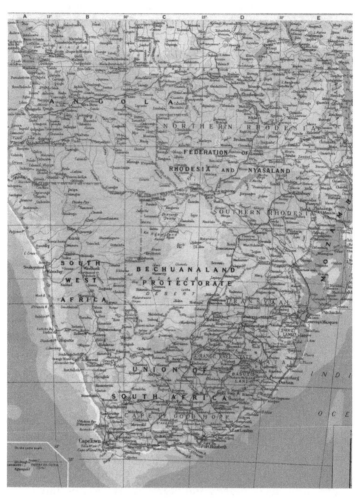

Southern Africa, circa 1956

AN ADVENTUROUS YOUTH

How on earth did I find myself living in the tropics, in Africa? The railways led me there, both metaphorically and physically, and how I became connected to the railways is a relatively straightforward story, which started when I was growing up. I was something of a disparate youth, restless and ebullient, to the extent that today I would no doubt have been diagnosed with ADHD or some similar condition. I was born reluctantly, or so it seems, in January 1929, some weeks late, in a rather sloppy mess on my mother's bed in a new post-slum clearance council house on The Manor Estate, Sheffield, England. I'm told my mother, Alice, was heard to say: "It's got a spout!" so there was immediate and crushing disappointment all round, right from the start, when it was clear that I was not the lovely little girl they'd all been hoping for. My only other sibling and first born son to my parents, Ronald, would therefore not have the little sister he had been promised.

My dad, Alf, was a deeply uncharitable and seriously parsimonious character, who dragged both meanness and selfishness in the human spirit to fantastical new lows. I don't think he ever gave me anything at all right up until the day he died, apart from the genes which have given me relative good health all my life. In mitigation I suppose we *were* very poor, certainly by today's standards, but I had no idea that I'd been born into a near permanent state of penury. You don't notice these things when you're a kid. Don't get me wrong, we never starved. We just didn't seem to have any money; at least it was the case that none ever came my way. It didn't bother me, as what you don't have you clearly don't miss, as the saying goes.

We kept our own chickens which lived very much with us in a large and quite malodorous wooden cupboard in the front room near the fireplace, so at least we almost always had fresh eggs. This was assuming no-one let the clucking birds out by mistake, an error which would then lead to front room chaos of pantomime proportions. My dad had to chase them around the ground floor of the house in his desperately inauspicious chicken-pursuit mode shouting: "Come 'ere ye little bastards!" or words to that effect, occasionally taking poorly aimed and obviously futile swipes at the mutinous escapees with a stair rod while clambering randomly all over the furniture. It made a welcome change from him whacking me with it I suppose, and it was quite good entertainment too, as there was no television in those days. I couldn't blame the poor chickens for sometimes wanting to hatch escape plans rather than eggs. They certainly caused major problems when they did escape, as there was insufficient space in the tiny room to dive full length at the errant, scheming birds. A decision had to be made very quickly when pouncing on them, whether to hit the wall or aim for the open fire. I remember on one occasion, while resolutely pursuing our cock bird around the house, my dad tripped over our bone-headed and snappy little Jack Russell dog and fell headlong into the fireplace. Luckily the fire wasn't lit at the time, as his head and shoulders plunged straight into the grate with such a thump that many years of soot came crashing down the chimney in one great, thunderous black cloud. After then managing to extricate himself from the chimney bottom and stand up, he turned around only to reveal to my absolute delight, and that of my brother, that he suddenly looked just like Al Jolson in full make-up, complete with black hands and face. He paused only briefly before continuing to chase the cock bird around the room, until it ran shrieking out the back door. On his return to the front room the terrified dog had relieved itself on the flock rug, probably in shock at being caught up in all the unexpected theatricals. My dad then ran into the kitchen and took hold of a towel that he'd cleverly fixed to the wooden draining board with a nail, and after folding it over several times placed it on the dog's steaming piss, then promptly started dancing around on it like he was practicing the quick step. Maybe he was. Outside the cock was sprinting around in the back yard and still had to be caught. Meanwhile the wind had got up and we suddenly heard two very loud bangs from the back door. My dad had fitted a home-made plywood storm door to the back door two days before, and the inner door had suddenly slammed shut in the wind. The new outer door then slammed hard and because it was constructed with my dad's usual expertise it immediately broke away from its hinges and fell into the back yard with a loud bang like a gun shot. Luckily it missed the cock, but crushed the neighbour's cat, which had seen the cock and had clearly decided to join in the pursuit. The poor moggy shrieked and squealed as only a cat can, before managing to drag itself away, bruised and bewildered. The next thing I knew I saw the same cat, apparently fit and well, pissing on my dad's carrots in the garden. It had clearly calculated the distance from its back end to the carrot tops in the ground, as the spray precisely covered each carrot perfectly. It had obviously done this before and was practiced at it. I later heard my dad tell my mum that it was good for the crop, as it helped prevent carrot fly.

I took every opportunity to absent myself from such a chaotic and dysfunctional house in order to do my own thing. I wanted to be out there, in the garden or in the street, or better still, in the fields at the back of our house, exploring. To me the world was our estate, and our part of Sheffield, and it demanded that I explore it. There was a huge sloping hill at the back of our house made entirely from waste coal, known as a 'slag heap', from a nearby coal mine. It was known colloquially as 'pit hill'. At the bottom of this huge, filthy slithering pile was a large accumulation of dangerously dirty stagnant water, known euphemistically as 'pit pond'. Nothing lived in it as it could support less life than The Dead Sea, but my pals and I frequently ended up immersed in it on occasions by accident when on our many adventures. This may, no doubt, be a probable cause of me once contracting scarlet fever and almost dying. In the pre-NHS days the doctor's bill took my parents years to pay off. I can only imagine Alf's initial reluctance to call a doctor in the first place, knowing he'd then have to pay for the visit. We used to slide down the full length of pit hill on sheets of razor-sharp corrugated iron, pulled erroneously by me from the roof of our wartime Anderson shelter in the back garden, trying our very best to avoid the pond, particularly in winter. It was great fun, made more so with the addition of deep snow on the hill which then increased our rate of descent several times over. My mates and I never gave any thought to the danger involved, until on one occasion I saw my own right hand disappear under the speeding sledge tearing it open as I sped along, unable to pull my arm out from underneath me until I came to a complete stop at the bottom. I was left with a huge gash which required six stitches, and a subsequent scar which I still have today.

All my spare time and thoughts were taken up with exploring pit hill and finding new ways to entertain myself and my mates. We lit fires in lorry tyres and sent them rolling at high speed down the hill, fully ablaze, in what must have been an incredibly dangerous and terrifying sight. One can only imagine the consequences of a huge, fully charged molten tyre hitting a human being, who was perhaps quietly walking their dog or stopping briefly to glance up the hill to hear what the screaming was about, the strange bouncing object heading silently towards them at high speed. We filled tin cans, usually old 'Oster milk' tins, with burning touchwood and coal and sent them flying high into the air on the end of a loop of steel wire. We called these 'winter warmers' and they looked absolutely spectacular, particularly at night, and were also no doubt potentially lethal. But our activities at the time were purely for our own amusement, and contained absolutely no element of premeditated malice whatsoever. I would imagine today the police would be called on any such antics and those involved dragged away for suitable punishment.

A little further down our street was a chap from India who we called 'Joe Bar'. He made kites from paper and bamboo canes and I bought one from him for four pennies. I'd just acquired the money from my friend Lacy Piggott's uncle, a soldier home on leave from India, and who was almost as dark skinned as Joe Bar. I've no idea why he gave me this money, other than the fact that I was Lacy's friend and he seemed to be an extremely generous man. They were brilliant kites and it wasn't long before I was making my own. My mates and I then had battles in the air with them, each with razor blades attached to the tips. It was spectacular fun. We once became very ambitious and made a huge kite with a span of twelve feet, the fore-runner of so many huge kites you can now see on wide summer beaches across the world. We only made one prototype though, because on its inaugural launch it took off in a favourable wind and my pal Billy was dragged screaming high into the air, landing with a spectacular but uncomfortable splash in the middle of pit pond. He gained revenge on me a few days later when we played 'walk as far as you can with your eyes shut'. He positioned me in the direction of my dad's timber and glass cucumber frame which I promptly fell headlong into, a large shard of glass missing my left eye by a fraction of an inch. More stitches required!

EMPLOYMENT

I was probably quite a clever, precocious lad, but my education didn't start very well. I clearly remember my first unforgettable day at school when I was five. I'd walked just a couple of hundred yards up Queen Mary Road to the top of the hill, and turned left past the formidable wrought-iron gates into the playground. I faced the darkly austere red brick building of The Manor Infants and Primary and was suddenly overcome with fear and reluctance. I was very apprehensive and so incredibly nervous that I promptly shit myself right there and then. I turned and ran crying all the way home, screaming like a banshee, solid bits of nervousness escaping my shorts and dropping down my legs, trailing all the way behind me. To my horror I found that no-one was home, and the house was locked, so I was forced to use my bare hands, some spit, and old newspaper from the bin to clean myself as best I could, still sobbing my heart out, sitting all alone on our front step. After a while I reluctantly walked back up the hill, fearing what my dad would do if he found out I hadn't been to school. I probably didn't smell particularly sweet on that first day.

When I eventually settled down and paid attention in class I really enjoyed it and achieved good results, regularly attaining 'A' grades in most subjects. I was frequently in competition with two others for the top marks, Renee James and Arthur Fox, and it became very competitive striving for the position as school swot. I passed my Eleven Plus exam and was destined for a grammar school, but this was not what I wanted, so I didn't go. I remember the headmaster of my school coming to our house and pleading with me and my mother to send me to a grammar school. I sat on the stairs, eyes glazed over with tears, sobbing wildly in an absurdly petulant display of stubbornness, refusing to accept their advice. Instead, at fourteen, I left school altogether. I wanted to be a milkman.

You just can't assess the true impact of decisions made in the past, but this one was probably not one of my best.

My first paid job was one I created myself. I collected potato peelings from anywhere I could and sold them to a nearby farmer. He fed the peelings to his pigs, and I remember on one occasion when I visited the farm he was in the process of castrating some of them. There was clearly no anaesthetic involved as I can never forgot the shrieks of pain from the pigs as the procedure was carried out, and the splashing of blood that followed. I helped my dad in the garden and in his greenhouse from an early age, and developed a life-long passion for gardening. I learned to grow a wide variety of plants and vegetables, and I have to admit that on reflection, Alf was quite good at growing most things, particularly tomatoes.

There was a world war happening around me at the time too, and because Sheffield was a major centre for steel production, the German Luftwaffe paid it particular attention. I remember frequently spending nights in our Anderson shelter in the back garden, before I'd ripped the roof off, listening for and counting the bombs as they fell. It was sheer terror as the line of falling bombs grew ever closer, and then luckily passed us by. It was just plain good luck that the bombs missed us the way they did. There's no doubt that if a 100lb bomb, dropped from a Heinkel high above, had landed anywhere near us it would have meant the end for us all, shelter or not. I swear I could hear my mother's heart beating loudly, over and above everything else in the damp and earthy darkness of the cramped shelter during the bombing. My mates and I spent hours collecting fragments of bomb shrapnel the day after each raid, comparing large jagged shards of metal which we found lying around all over the place.

Just after Christmas 1942 I finally became a milkman when I sat in the front of a truck as a driver's mate, collecting milk churns from Derbyshire dairy farms. I helped in the pasteurisation and bottling process too and thoroughly enjoyed myself. Then in 1945 I became suddenly impatient with my wonderful job as a milkman and quite on a whim, and I've no idea why, I bought a one penny platform ticket, walked up to the station master's office at Sheffield's main Victoria railway station and asked for a job.

The Station Master was a hugely corpulent, Mr Bumble character who wore a dark, ill-fitting three-piece suit, with a gold pocket watch chain which hung brightly across his prominently rounded belly. He wore a dusty black bowler hat, even indoors, and never seemed to take it off. On the rare occasions that I saw him stand up from behind his huge leather-topped desk, the act of which he clearly found a tremendous effort, I often heard the subtle but distinct sound of accidental flatulence emanating from his massive backside. Clearly audible to anyone in the vicinity, he would then cough slightly, one hand raised to his mouth in a clenched fist, and proclaim: "Must get that floor board sorted out, young Dennis!" and carry on his work. He was possessed of an extremely bright red face, booming voice and for some reason he immediately took pity on me.

I was set to work as a junior parcel porter. I had to make tea amongst many other important duties, and take the Station Master his lunch on a silver tray, some of which he occasionally left, telling me I could finish it off if I wanted. Again, I've no idea whether this was from genuine benevolence or simple pity. I had to sort the mail into pigeon holes, and saw the place names of dozens of towns and cities in Britain and abroad which sparked a curiosity for travel and adventure. There was clearly much more to the world than Sheffield. Quite soon I was promoted to the position of 'TR Boy', which meant Train Register Boy. I then worked in a large signal box and part of my duties were to record every passing train, which was very often quite demanding. I also worked on the station platform and managed to quickly acquire a thorough knowledge of the train movements and timings. I perhaps became a little too confident, as on one occasion I strode rather grandly down the full length of the platform in my resplendent TR Boy uniform shouting: "All change!" banging on the windows of the stationary train, instructing all the passengers to alight from the carriages, including First Class, who then dragged themselves and all their expensive bags reluctantly out onto the platform, only to be followed fifty yards behind by the Station Inspector who was shouting: "Get back in! Get back in!" to all the passengers. Sadly, to my horror, I hadn't noticed there had been a last minute change in the schedule.

I thoroughly enjoyed my job and despite some occasional embarrassing mistakes I was encouraged to take my exams for the clerical grade. I was, at first, reluctant to do this, as it was a major step up the scale, and was usually reserved for grammar school boys. There was very much a 'know your place' ethos in the UK at the time, with a very rigid class system, and any deviation from the norm was frowned upon. Indeed, when I took the exam it was in the company of some rather posh young men who, it seemed, didn't feel as though they should lower themselves to even make conversation with me. But I passed the exam and interview quite easily and was duly promoted to clerical grade. I then spent twelve months taking evening classes in 'The Rudiments of Railway Law' at Sheffield University. I also found time to have occasional piano lessons.

After the war my railway career was sadly suspended for two years while I served King and Country in my National Service, starting in 1947. It wasn't until then that my penurious upbringing became truly evident. I've always joked that until I joined the army I'd never worn underpants or possessed a toothbrush. It seems peculiar now, and amusing, in a sad kind of way, but it was true.

After the army, I knew I should pursue a career which I'd enjoyed before my National Service. My experience and confidence in the railways therefore prompted me to take a train to Manchester and to the Midland Hotel, for an interview. There was a vacancy for a job in the Rhodesia Railways.

MANCHESTER

At this point I began to feel slightly uneasy about my future intentions. After I'd waved goodbye to my girlfriend, Esther, at the station in Sheffield, and I was alone, my thoughts began to wander as I stared out of the carriage window. Then as the smoke-filled and over-crowded train clattered along towards Manchester on that grey day of early autumn, the closer it came to the final destination the more nervous I felt. Years had passed since that fateful first day of school, but I couldn't help fighting back similar emotions, and I hoped above all else that I'd be able to maintain adequate control of my bowels. I was attending an interview for a job in Africa, not a job on a milk round, or on the platform at Sheffield's Victoria station. I felt way out of my depth, and struggled to resist the temptation to turn back and not even go to the interview. People from my background just didn't go gallivanting across the globe thinking they were intrepid world explorers. We should know our place and be satisfied with our lot, working down the pit or the steelworks and staying put for ever, living and dying within a few miles of where we'd grown up. This was what was entirely expected of me, and nothing more. I was defying convention, a lad from The Manor Estate thinking he could better himself in such a way. The furthest I'd been away from home prior to my time in the army was a week with my family in The Isle of Man when I was ten, mysteriously financed by some sort of win connected with Littlewoods, the football pools people. I hadn't been far with the army either, so Africa really did seem to be a place at the other end of the earth. At any moment I expected to wake up from this delusion, and return home to Ma and Pa, Ron, the chickens and our Jack Russell dog.

The Midland Hotel, Manchester, is only a short walk from the main railway station, and still stands today, prominent and angular on a busy corner in the city centre, like the bow of some enormous ship. It was, and still is, a huge, palatial pre-possessing Victorian construction, in smooth red brick with hundreds of arched windows and rows of tall chimney pots on the roof. The entrance lobby at that time was cavernous and very grand, and I strode towards the reception desk trying my utmost not to feel intimidated by my surroundings. Before I reached the desk I heard my name called in a vaguely familiar voice from the other end of the lobby:

"Dennis, over here, how are you?"

I turned and saw John Brandt, a man who I'd met briefly on a few occasions at Victoria station in Sheffield and who had initially encouraged me to apply for the job. He walked over to me and grabbed my hand, shaking it firmly, while smiling very warmly.

"Hello," I said, "nice to see you again," quite relieved to see a familiar face. His smooth bald head shone in the bright lights of the lobby, and I noticed he seemed to be wearing the same expensive-looking suit that he always wore. He was Rhodesian, lean and tanned, the skin on his face was lined and creased like the elbow of a well-worn leather coat, as though previously exposed to far too many days of hot sun but now fading rapidly to a pale pallor more appropriate to the damp English climate.

"Splendid, Dennis, splendid!" he replied in his clipped South African accent, still shaking my hand, while peering straight into my eyes. He turned me deftly around and led me away from the reception desk towards some imposing double doors off the main lobby. I was ushered through these huge doors and into a long and brightly lit conference room, with a highly polished rectangular table in the centre running almost the full length of the room, lined all around with heavy dark wood chairs. Two other men walked in after us and I was introduced to these, also both Rhodesians. We sat in a close group at one end of the vast table and drank coffee before a meal was served. The food consisted of salad with Scottish salmon, and I remember thinking my portion of fish was cold and seemed to be completely uncooked. I briefly noticed theirs appeared the same, and they ate it without comment, so I tucked into mine too. I wondered if I'd be ill later, from eating what was clearly raw fish.

I was beginning to feel more at ease as the many terms and conditions of the job were then discussed. It was certainly not a conventional interview. All three Rhodesians alternately smiled, then looked very serious as they explained the position, the lifestyle, and what was expected of me. My excitement grew as they informed me that all my travelling expenses to Rhodesia would be paid, and in addition I would be given a 'sub' – some subsistence cash – on arrival in Cape Town.

"You will love it out there, Dennis, you really will," one of them said, and I noticed his teeth were as white as his blonde hair. He went on: "Do you have a girlfriend? Bring her with you to Rhodesia, all expenses paid, get married and become Rhodesian citizens, serving King and Empire!"

It felt as though I'd already been given the job, and the idea of taking Esther with me was hugely tempting. But this was an adventure I felt I needed to do alone, and I doubted if she would be willing to come along, so far from home. After the meal another coffee was served and the conversation became lighter and less specific. I was offered a taxi back to the station but declined; it was only a short walk away.

"Wait for a formal letter offering you the job, Dennis," John said, "and then you are on your way!"

The train journey back to Sheffield was filled with enormous trepidation and excitement.

LONDON

With little surprise, within a week my letter of appointment duly arrived with all travel instructions. Just before midnight on Wednesday 22nd November 1950, I said goodbye to Esther and boarded the train to London. We had agreed that we would carry on our relationship from this point when I returned, and if not, then fate would decide. My mind was in turmoil. I didn't want to leave Esther, and I believed we had a future together, but this was an opportunity to earn a great deal of money, which on my return would be a huge help in getting ourselves started in life.

As the London train gathered speed in the darkness I became terribly introspective, as my own reflection peered back at me mockingly in the darkened window. Was I happy, confused, or just plain mad? What would I find in Africa? Would I even return to Sheffield? I remembered my dad's farewell comment a few hours before, spoken in his true Yorkshire vernacular:

"Weer's tha' goin'?"

"Africa," I replied.

"Oh…" he said, bending over to put another lump of coal on the fire. A few minutes later he was buttoning up his coat in silence and was gone, the front door banging loudly behind him as he trudged off to work as usual at the furnaces in the huge Firth Brown steelworks in Sheffield's east end. I don't remember saying goodbye to my mother and brother, but I suppose I did.

The train was travelling faster now, faster than any train I'd been on, pulling me further and further away from home. I remembered how the speed could be calculated by listening to the clackety-clack of the wheels on the track, and I thought of the young TR Boy I'd just seen at Sheffield station, how he must have been on his night shift, a shift I used to enjoy. I wondered if he was busy, as busy as I was when I did the same job only a few years before. I wondered if he helped himself to fresh produce on the goods trains, and if he ever saw the gorgeous, mouth-watering grapes in the boxes marked 'Cape', and whether he ate a few from one of the many damaged boxes as I had. Did this TR Boy ever stumble on couples engaged in frantic, illicit sex in the dark corners of quiet goods vans? I wondered if he was ever enrolled as I was into helping scrape the remains of bodies from the roof and sides of the train carriages, the remnants of unfortunate souls either deliberately or accidentally departed this earth in extreme and shocking suddenness.

I eventually fell asleep. When I woke up, minutes or hours later, I've no idea how long, nothing had changed. I was still sitting in the dimly lit, stale-smelling carriage, opposite an assortment of grim, poker-faced fellow passengers. Drifting in and out of sleep for the next few hours, the train hissed and belched to a stop in Marylebone Station in clouds of smoke and steam. The carriage I was in suddenly erupted into life as everyone tried to be the first to get off the train. I knew I had several hours to kill so I took my time collecting my two cases from the luggage van. I felt a surge of pride as I picked them up, as both were marked: 'CAPE TOWN' and 'HOLD' in giant red letters. I wondered whether or not I was in a dream, or a nightmare. I took a taxi to Waterloo station and found a quiet bench to sit on, my two cases gathered closely around my feet. The 'Boat Train' to Southampton was due to leave at 12.45pm. I still had a few hours to wait.

I've no doubt that I looked naïve and anxious, and this would probably explain why I was approached at about 9.30am that morning, and was so attractive to the tall, friendly chap I spent the next few hours in company with. I first noticed him when he appeared next to the bench I was sitting on and just stood there for a few moments before moving closer to me.

"Hello young man! A fellow sea-going adventurer I see from your luggage, Cape Town eh?"

He moved parallel to me and said: "May I sit?" just as he

then sat himself down next to me, close enough to be attentive, but not overwhelming. He spoke well, he was well dressed and patrician in his manner, and I made my best efforts to speak and behave in a way befitting his company, as he was obviously a man of wealth and high social standing. I immediately told him precisely what he needed to know, that I was a very inexperienced traveller, and was excited yet apprehensive about travelling to South Africa on my own. I noticed he then glanced around quickly as though confirming I was alone, and I went on to inform him that except for my National Service army days when I hadn't travelled very far at all, the furthest I'd ever been before was the Isle of Man. I recounted how seasick I'd been on the relatively short sea crossing and he seemed very interested and promised he would bring me warm soup on the voyage to Cape Town, telling me: "It works wonders old boy," and: "done it a dozen times," and so on. I felt relieved that I'd found someone, or more accurately someone had found me, who would be able to assist me on my travels. I began to feel a little more relaxed.

"Allow me to introduce myself," he said, reaching into his suit pocket and handing me a smart business card, "Digby Caruthers, Director of the South African Mining Corporation."

I was impressed, and yet more impressed by all the letters after his name on the card. I thanked providence for sending me such invaluable assistance, just at a time when I was very low and needed it the most.

"Come on," he said, standing up and beckoning me towards him, "I know a jolly nice coffee house near Bush House in the Strand, I'll take you there and we can have a coffee, on me of course!"

I was swept along by this man's apparent good nature and enthusiasm, so I stood up immediately and found myself walking with him out of the station. I handed both my cases into 'Left Luggage' on the way out, at Mr Caruthers's insistence.

"I have some business to conclude, a jolly enormous contract, then we can have a good old chin-wag about our trip to Cape Town, eh?" he was smiling very energetically and bounded along the pavement, as though in a tearing hurry, and I struggled to keep up. The streets of London in early winter 1950 were depressingly dull and grey. Everything was still rationed despite the war having ended more than five years before. It really was a continuing time of extreme austerity. Young people today joke that everything in those days appeared to be in black and white and dreary, but on this particular day they wouldn't have been far wrong. It was cold and overcast, and by today's standards the roads were relatively quiet, both in vehicular and pedestrian traffic.

It was quite a walk to Bush House, but sure enough, there was the coffee house my new friend had spoken about, and he bought me a very agreeable cup of hot, sweet coffee, which I enjoyed tremendously. Again I thought how lucky I was to be in his company. After the coffee we walked to Bush House.

"Wait here old chap, I've just got to pop inside and sign the contract and hand them my cheque for the wax seal, and then I'll be right with you!" He promptly disappeared up the front stone steps and through the swing doors into Bush House. I stood there waiting patiently, occasionally glancing around and into the lobby to see if he would reappear. Finally when he came out after almost half an hour he looked flustered and anxious.

"The rotters won't accept a cheque for the seal on the contract, you haven't got five pounds have you old chap, just until I can call at my bank on the way back to Waterloo?"

I reached inside my pocket for my wallet. Five pounds was *all* I had, apart from a small amount of loose change. It was intended to last me the whole two week voyage to Cape Town. I handed him my precious and hard-earned five pound note. He turned and ran back through the swing doors. By this time my train was due to leave in less than an hour.

I waited again, becoming ever more anxious. After another half an hour there was no sign of Mr Caruthers. Eventually I walked up the steps and through the doors into the lobby of Bush House. There was no-one about, except for a female cleaner busily washing the tiled floor with a mop, the end of a cigarette dangling from her tightly pursed lips.

"Excuse me, have you seen my friend, a well-dressed chap, came in here about half an hour ago?"

"Yes I seen 'im," replied the cleaner, drawing the mop closer to her, then standing still, leaning on it heavily with both hands. She paused, looked around idly and then stared directly at me. "I seen 'im twice as a matter of fact. The second time was about 'alf an hour ago, peculiar it was. He just come runnin' in the front and went straight out the back door there, into the street and gorn 'e was. He never stopped or nuffin'." She nodded her head in the direction of the back door to the foyer. It was an ugly, shabby little back door. He clearly did not have a business deal to clinch of any sort.

I suddenly felt physically sick. He was 'gorn' and probably by now miles away with *my* five pound note. I felt my whole body starting to shake, and my heart dropped like a brick through the freshly cleaned floor. I realised what had happened.

"'Ere, are you alright?" the cleaner inquired, obviously seeing me trembling as though about to collapse. I couldn't answer; I just looked blankly around me, trying to take in what I'd done. Then to add to my problems I saw the clock on the wall in the lobby mocking me, telling me I had less than thirty minutes before my train left for Southampton. I was suddenly running out of time. It was at least twenty minutes' walk back to Waterloo. Forcing back my tears and a very deep desire just to forget it all and head for home, I ran through the streets of London towards Waterloo. Not daring to look at any clocks on the way I contemplated leaving my luggage, thinking I wouldn't have time to collect it.

I dashed past The Strand cinema and briefly noticed they were showing the film *In a Lonely Place* with Humphrey Bogart, and I remember thinking this was exactly where I was that moment. I skidded into the Left Luggage office in my leather shoes only to find an elderly woman at the counter in front of me who seemed to be in the process of collecting all the world's luggage, and as slowly as she possibly could, from one single member of staff on duty. I begged her to hurry and must have seemed incredibly anxious and rude just as another chap appeared behind the counter and handed me my cases, having luckily remembered me from earlier. I heard him shout behind me: "Have a good trip young man!" as I ran out the office and onto the platform.

I threw my cases into the luggage van at the rear of the train, and then dived into a compartment just as I heard the guard blow his whistle. I collapsed into my seat, physically exhausted and mentally traumatised from being conned out of virtually all my money. I was chuntering to myself, cursing over and over at how stupid I'd been. This could not get any worse. I vowed I would never trust anyone again, however convivial and genuine they seemed. I would never make friends again or allow anyone to befriend me in such a manner.

As I gathered my breath I looked up and saw an outstretched hand from a smiling passenger opposite me:

"Hello, I'm Fred, Fred Leach, pleased to meet you…"

THE CAPETOWN CASTLE

Fred Leach was an irresistible companion. Despite my recent vows to avoid doing so, friendship seemed inevitable with Fred very soon after we struck up our first conversation. I had no idea at the time where this friendship would lead, but we gelled from the very start. I told him of my meeting with Mr Caruthers and he found it absolutely hilarious. I know he tried in vain to keep a straight face at first while I was recounting what happened, but then he just couldn't restrain himself, particularly at the point where the cleaner told me about Caruthers running straight out the back door. He even managed to convince *me* there was a funny side to it.

To my amazement it seemed we were both destined for jobs in the Rhodesia Railways and it was at that point that he very generously loaned me five pounds for the voyage, which I found particularly touching. Few people had been as kind to me before, to this extent, and so readily. We knew we were to receive some money from our employers when we arrived in Cape Town, so I would be able to pay him back straight away. Fred was similar in size and stature to me, about 5'8" tall, slim, thick dark hair, and good looking. He was from Manchester, but to me he had no discernible accent of any sort. He told me bluntly however, that my Yorkshire accent was very noticeable, despite spending two years in the army. It seemed we had similar backgrounds, but Fred was reluctant to discuss his home life in detail, that is until later in the voyage.

We followed everyone else from the train, dragging our luggage along like a stream of refugees. We found *The Capetown Castle* and walked up the gang plank onto the ship together. Fred and I were both equally mesmerised by what we saw. Though it was by now becoming quite dark I could see the side of the ship was a very pale lavender colour and looked absolutely brand new. To us it was as though we were stepping aboard the *Titanic*, the ship just seemed so huge and luxurious. All the passengers on board the ship – and there seemed to be hundreds of them – were very smartly dressed and were clearly wealthy people, quite a distinct contrast from Fred and I. I was beginning to catch my first glimpse into another way of life, and I found it beguiling and irresistible in equal measure.

The interior of the ship was beautiful, with shiny floors, highly polished wood and glistening brass everywhere. As I walked aboard I noticed a strong smell of Brasso mixed with stale cigars and some very subtle but not unpleasant cooking smells. *The Royal Mail Motor Vessel Capetown Castle* was part of a fleet of similar ships of the Union-Castle Line which sailed to South Africa on a regular published schedule. The fare, so I was told, should have been around £50, which was a huge sum of money at the time. It had been a troop ship during the war and had undergone a major refurbishment in 1947.By bizarre coincidence this was the exact same ship my elder brother Ron had sailed on to the Middle East towards the end of World War Two, when he was flying in Liberators as a gunner.

At exactly four o'clock, on Thursday 23rd November, I could feel the gentle vibration from the engines deep inside the ship churning into life and we started to move inch by gentle inch away from the quay side. All the excited passengers leaned against the railings and threw handfuls of white streamers down onto the quay, perhaps at friends and relatives, and there was a huge amount of waving, shouting and cheering both from the deck and back up from the quay. Fred and I were not party to this, and could only look on in wide-eyed amazement.

As our very elegant vessel gained speed and pulled away from Southampton people on deck began to disperse, chattering and laughing, then heading downstairs to their cabins. Thousands of the thin paper streamers clung to the port side railings, and young crewmen walked up and down gathering them up in their arms, stuffing them into canvas sacks on straps around their shoulders as they did so.

We descended the stairs below and discovered, to our

astonishment, that Fred and I each had our own en-suite cabins, with our own individual porthole view of the sea. My cabin wasn't huge but still seemed absolutely luxurious. There was a crisp, clean feel to the inside, as it was almost entirely decorated and furnished in white, with white walls and fresh white linen on the bed. The en-suite had a bath with alternative fresh water or salt water taps. I remember thinking: *I'm going to like this!*

My cabin was Number 30, and was on the same side of the same corridor as Fred in Number 50. He knocked on my door just before seven o'clock, as arranged, so we could both go to dinner together. Up the stairs and into the 'saloon', we noticed a sign by the door which stated: '*Passengers are kindly requested to refrain from smoking in the saloon.*' Neither Fred nor I smoked, so it was of no concern to us. As soon as we walked in we were pounced upon by a very smartly dressed and attentive waiter in a brilliant white uniform who asked us for our cabin numbers, whether we wanted to dine together, to which we agreed, and then politely showed us to a table.

We seemed to be dining in a very smart restaurant, and as I sat down I noticed a small paper menu on the table. It looked as though it had been written by someone with only a partial knowledge of French and no confidence in the use of it. There was: '*Garden peas a la menthe*' and '*Sued Oise au cerise*', whatever that was. I understood the part about the garden peas. We didn't have to wait long before our waiter brought us a huge round plate each with a large rolled up piece of fish in the middle, all on its own. We were then served some garden peas and waited a while for the accompanying chips, but they never came. Other people were already eating so we decided to tuck in. The peas had a strange minty flavour and were quite nice, as was the fish, but I missed a large portion of chips! The moment we'd cleared our plates they were whisked away and the next course from the menu arrived: '*Trenton of Cape sole au citron avec braised onions, demi-glace, and a cushion of veal.*' I have to say that it was all very nice, and both Fred and I completely cleared our plates. We'd just left the austerity of

England during rationing, so this was unbelievable food. Dessert followed, and coffee. The coffee was very dark, incredibly strong, and had a deeply rich flavour such as I'd never tasted before.

To use modern parlance, Fred and I were at the bottom of a very steep learning curve. We felt very different to everyone else on the ship and we joked during the meal as to whether we'd been rumbled, and they all knew we were not really part of this social set. But then we were there, and we had to learn how to swim amongst these big fish as best we could. We followed some other people and took our coffee into the adjoining lounge area. We sat in some huge comfortable armchairs and people-watched for a while. Smartly dressed men and women lit cigarettes as soon as they emerged from the saloon restaurant and made their way past us and outside onto the deck, laughing and joking hysterically as though they hadn't a care in the world. Perhaps they hadn't. After coffee Fred and I made our way towards the bow of the ship but were turned away from some parts by signs saying: *'First Class Only'*. This was where most of the activity and noise seemed to be coming from. So we stood at the stern of the ship for a while, watching the churning of the sea in the wake of the propellers, and as the ship seemed to cut effortlessly through the ocean ever faster, the smooth movement and long trail of white water seemed to emphasise the distance we were putting between us and dear old Blighty. I then had some twinges of homesickness, and thoughts of my girlfriend, Esther. I had nagging doubts as to whether I'd done the right thing by leaving.

I'd not slept much in the previous twenty-four hours so I returned to my cabin quite early. I had a relaxing bath and climbed into my crisp, clean sheets. I reflected on the day and felt incredibly lucky and relaxed. I was probably asleep in a few short moments, the gentle throb of the ship's engines no doubt having a soporific effect on me.

I was up and on deck at eight o'clock the next morning. Fred came up to me while I was leaning on the rail overlooking the sea, smiling broadly. He shook my hand warmly as though we were best of friends reunited after months apart. Breakfast was served at eight-thirty and we entered the saloon together. We laughed at the name 'saloon' and from then on every time we walked in Fred would say to me: "After you, amigo!" perhaps acknowledging so many old cowboy films where the saloon played such a pivotal role in the story. This saloon was certainly no exception. The breakfasts were superb. It was in a buffet style, and today would probably be known as an all-inclusive 'all you can eat' meal. There were kippers, full English breakfast of sausages, eggs, bacon, with toast and as much tea, coffee or fruit juice as you could drink: exceptional food for such austere times.

That night, when we started to cross the Bay of Biscay, I began to feel terribly seasick. I just managed to reach my cabin before I was violently sick in the toilet. Fred came down to see me but there was nothing anyone could do. I needed a couple of days in order to acquire my 'sea legs'. It wasn't even as if the sea was wildly rolling and tossing *The Capetown Castle* around, it wasn't, but it really was noticeable how it had started to pitch and roll much more once we'd left the relative calm of the English Channel. I missed the evening meal that night and wondered if there had been any truth in Digby Caruthers's claim that soup would help. But then everything he had told me had probably been a lie.

That night I didn't sleep much at all. It was punctuated by frequently having to crawl on all fours out of my bed across the floor of the cabin and sticking my head in the toilet. I spent all night talking to God Almighty on the big white telephone. I must have done this at least a dozen times during the night. Eventually, through a bleary-eyed haze, I noticed it was daylight, only because the porthole in my cabin was no longer inky black. I'd wretched time and again until there was nothing left inside. All the next day I was the same. Fred was very concerned and came into my cabin with a medical officer who gave me some seasickness calming tablets. I was very sceptical but that night I slept much better and rarely had to repeat the previous night's antics.

On the morning of the third day, after being confined to my cabin for forty-eight hours solid, I emerged on deck feeling as delicate as a priceless vase, but very relieved and hungry. I sat on deck with Fred sipping a very sweet coffee, and it tasted superb. I'd missed breakfast so lunch was my first meal in two days. Whether it was the passage of time, or the tablets I'd been given, or both, I was never seasick again on that voyage. As I recovered I began to thoroughly enjoy my surroundings. I couldn't help but think to myself how lucky I was to be there, and my excitement grew about the whole adventure.

On the fourth day we docked in Las Palmas in the Canary Islands for a few hours. Most of the passengers, including Fred and I, stood on deck, gazing across at the town, while local boys dived for coins thrown over the side by people leaning over the railings. The water was crystal clear and very deep, but few – if any – coins were lost. We didn't disembark, but small liberty boats brought mail and food to the ship, including huge amounts of fresh fruit. I couldn't believe the size and variety of fruit that was brought aboard and which we would later see on the tables in the saloon. The clear blue sea lapped gently against the dock and in the town the buildings looked clean and white, with enormous palm trees here and there swaying majestically in a fantastic warm breeze. Other passengers were wandering around the deck and we sat for a while in deckchairs overlooking the quay, drinking coffee.

Las Palmas looked spectacular and eventually we could see the final provisions being loaded aboard, and the single low funnel began emitting the occasional thin brown puff of smoke into the still air. The calm silence changed to a low rumble when the ship's engines fired into life and more smoke started rising from the funnel. It was a beautifully warm day, and in late afternoon the sun ebbed lower in a vast cloudless sky, then gradually changed colour to form a deepening orange ball, which seemed to simply melt away into the distant ocean.

Once under way again Fred and I sat in our deckchairs staring out to sea, watching the remains of the sunset. We talked in great depth about home. I told him about Esther and he told me about his home life, and the main reason why he'd left England. He said he never knew his father; he didn't have any other siblings, and so all he had was his mother. She had started a relationship with a man who by all accounts sounded like a violent alcoholic. He had tried to protect his mother, whom he clearly worshipped, and make the best of an awful situation but it just didn't work. He became tearful at this point, so I didn't press him any further. I changed the subject and told him of my experience on the railways and I asked him what he was going to do in Africa. He said he'd just become a qualified accountant, and so this was the position he'd been interviewed for in the Rhodesia Railways. This was also when Fred told me he had become teetotal. We both managed a chuckle of relief when I told him I was too!

There were deck games on the ship, and a small swimming pool at the bow, for the free use of all the passengers. There seemed to be other nocturnal games on the ship too, but in the middle of the night, and on most nights. I heard frequent banging of cabin doors on our corridor to the extent that one night at three o'clock in the morning when it was particularly noisy, I decided I would open my door slightly to take a look. What I witnessed was like a scene from a music hall farce, as scantily clad men and women, and some completely naked, darted across the corridor from room to room, clearly making full use of the ship, and each other, twenty-four hours a day!

I'd heard rumours of a 'Crossing the Line' ceremony when the ship passed the equator. About a week into the voyage a very formal notice appeared on the deck notice board asking for the names of anyone interested in celebrating the 'crossing of the line'. Of course Fred and I eagerly put our names down, along with quite a few others. We were not sure what it was about but we knew the pool was somehow involved, and we were joined in our conversation by two other men who seemed to be the same age as Fred and I. John 'Taffy' Williams and Bill Hinds were in a similar situation to us, and were heading for work in Salisbury and Bulawayo respectively. It was great to meet some other blokes on the ship we had something in common with. Fred told me he was worried about being thrown into the pool as he claimed he was not a strong swimmer, a claim that was refuted before my eyes months later in Africa.

The next day the 'Crossing the Line' ceremony took place. I volunteered to be first. Chairs had been lined up by the pool and dozens of people stood around watching and cheering. I was sitting in my chair in a pair of shorts and a short-sleeved shirt facing the pool, when I suddenly felt some warm sloppy dampness on my head and around my neck. I touched it with my hand to see it was a strange brown liquid, and I was being covered with buckets of the stuff. I was then spattered with white foam all over until I was almost completely covered, much to the amusement of everyone gathered around. Then my chair was lifted up at the back and I was tipped into the pool, to more hilarity and a round of applause. I'd joined the 'Crossing the Line Club'. Fred, Taffy, Bill and several others followed, and there was a fantastic atmosphere. Fred luckily survived the dunking without a problem.

That night we were informed of another crossing, this time 'the crossing of the ships', as a sister ship of *The Capetown Castle*, *The Stirling Castle*, came steaming past us silently and majestically in the opposite direction, both ships being only a few hundred yards apart. The ships were brightly lit and each vessel sounded its horn and people on the decks of both cheered and waved. It was a wonderful sight. This was not our last contact with other vessels. A couple of days later in the middle of the night I sensed the engines had stopped and an unusual, eerie silence followed. I could tell immediately that the ship had come to a stop, but it was unscheduled, and we were in the middle of the ocean, as earlier the same day there had been no sign of land from anywhere on the ship. I left my cabin to see what was happening. I was shocked to see a small boat was being lowered by some of our crew, and it appeared to be a lifeboat. Other passengers gathered and insisted on knowing what was happening. The small boat touched the water far below and a motor was started. It was steered away from our ship at ninety degrees and disappeared into the night. Then I saw some lights bobbing around in the near distance, from another, smaller ship. Half an hour later our little boat came back, with one extra passenger. It seemed a tramp steamer had radioed for help, as they had a sick crewman on board. *The Capetown Castle* had a doctor and some first class medical facilities, which was reassuring to know, so we took the poor man with us. I never did find out what happened to him, or even what was wrong with him.

CAPE TOWN: INTO AFRICA

In the final few days aboard the ship I sat on deck with my three new friends in the sunshine. We talked with great enthusiasm about what lay ahead for each of us. There was some apprehension of course, but so far we were enjoying an adventure that was exceeding all our expectations. After two weeks at sea we finally arrived at Cape Town. Tugs came alongside and fussed around us like bees around their queen and hauled us slowly up to the quayside. I saw Table Mountain for the first time, high above the city, and my first thoughts were just how incredible Cape Town looked with such spectacular background scenery. It was truly wonderful. Then I thought how bright and clean everything appeared, just as it did in Las Palmas. There were no dark and dismal streets of dreary back-to-back houses shrouded in winter fog and industrial pollution. It was early summer, it was very warm, and there were date palms swaying in a gentle breeze. Even the air seemed to be lightly perfumed and smelt sweet and pure.

We disembarked from the ship with our luggage and assembled on the quay. Fred pulled out his camera and took a few photographs and quite soon we were joined by two officials from the Rhodesia Railways who took us in a large taxi into the town. The streets of Cape Town near the docks were wide and wonderful, lined with palm trees and spotlessly clean and tidy. In the city centre, green and white double-decker buses were driven around on the same side of the road as in England and there were immaculate landscaped gardens and lawns in front of grand colonial buildings. I noticed however, that to say we had arrived in Africa, I saw surprisingly few black people.

We arrived at a large old hotel in the city centre and were escorted into a conference room, much like the one in the Midland Hotel in Manchester. We were each given quite a large amount of cash in sterling, and a sealed envelope containing joining and appointment instructions for when we arrived at our ultimate destination. We were told our train north was at four-thirty and informed how to get to the station, and that was it, very brief and to the point. I handed Fred a crisp five pound note, with my thanks, and we started to make our way to the railway station.

It was a short journey on foot to the station, and as we walked I noticed ominous and peculiar signs everywhere in shop doorways: 'WHITES ONLY'. At first sight I didn't understand what they meant, but then I realised why I'd not seen many native black people. They were clearly not welcome as most buildings were forbidden to them. This was Afrikaner country: fiercely proud white South Africans, many of whom were descended from the original Dutch settlers, the Boers, who spoke a dialect known as Afrikaans, a bastardised form of Dutch. We walked through the market and acting on impulse I bought a clothes brush, I've no idea why. I think it was something of a novelty, as I'd never seen one before. I also bought an enormous pineapple, for the same reason, and I was very curious to see what I could do with it!

Cape Town was where the headquarters of the South African Railways was located, and the main station reflected this with a rather grand and spacious interior. Inside it reeked of the foul smelling South African cigarettes most people seemed to smoke, and it was a massive contrast to the sweet fresh air outside. Our train arrived and we boarded, finding seats around a table in the through-coach, with four seats around each table, two on each side by the window. The train lurched forward and heaved its way slowly out of the station just on time, in thick clouds of black-grey smoke. It just managed to achieve a brisk walking pace by the time we'd left the confines of the station, but then it didn't seem to gain any speed at all after that.

We began to relax in our seats, and once out of the city we passed lush green fields lined in neat rows with grape vines leading far into the distance towards the mountains. These were the 'Cape' grapes I used to occasionally plunder from the broken boxes when I worked as TR Boy years before. Who would have guessed then that I would now be looking at the very place where they were grown!

Taffy, Bill, Fred and I were staring at my pineapple on the table as it occasionally rolled around in front of us when Taffy finally said: "Well, are you going to do something with that, Dennis?"

I had no idea how to attack it, and with only one small pen-knife between us that Bill had extricated from one of his pockets, it was decided to cut it in two first. We then took turns in cutting the fruit from inside, and as we did so the juice poured out of it all over the table and onto the floor. After much slithering and sliding about on the wooden table to the amused consternation of some other passengers, we managed to cut it roughly into four untidy segments and chewed our way through the majority of it. It was very sweet and refreshing. I brought some toilet paper back from the train lavatory and mopped up the sticky mess. In the meantime our train was struggling up an incline and our speed had deteriorated even further. We all agreed, as railway men, that the train should have had a 'banker', another engine at the back to assist, as many trains in the UK had. But at least at that speed we could really appreciate the passing scenery, and it was becoming quite spectacular. Mountains in the distance were high enough to be covered in wispy strips of thin cloud, and we seemed to be passing through mile after endless mile of grape vines.

There was no dining car on the train, no sleeping facilities other than the seats we were occupying, and we could not access our luggage as it was at the back of the train secured in the luggage van. This meant we would remain in the same clothes for the entire journey, however long it was going to be. After a couple of hours, and as it grew quickly dark, the train began to pick up speed a little as the ground around us flattened out. One after the other we started to fall asleep until I noticed I was the last to nod off. Eventually the gentle swaying of the carriage and the *clack-clack* from the track below sent me into a deep sleep too. We all slept soundly in our seats that first night, quite exhausted from our arrival in Cape Town and the sight-seeing in the city.

As the early morning light filled the carriage I opened my eyes and noticed the scenery was becoming less lush and the open spaces spread out far into the distance. I could see the others around our little table were equally captivated by the view, and conversation was minimal. We trundled along, hour after hour, now making quite a good speed, with nothing but vast expanses of emptiness out the window of the train on either side.

Our first major stop was a town called Kimberley, which was about 500 miles north of Cape Town. We were informed we had a couple of hours to stretch our legs, so we gladly jumped down off the train and walked a short distance into the town. To describe Kimberley as a town was probably being a little over generous at that time. It reminded me of a desperate, wind-swept frontier town in the cowboy films of the Old West. We walked into a hotel bar and this was even more like the Wild West. A highly polished, dark wood bar with a brass handrail ran the full length of an enormous room, with some huge, very untidy rough-looking white men with leathery brown faces seated on bar stools sipping beer from half-pint glasses. The barman was standing behind the bar in front of some enormous mirrors and looked as fat and sweaty as most of his customers. He stood with an apron around him, stained and dirty, stereotypically drying a glass, giving us a very quizzical and faintly hostile look. It seemed he might pull out a shotgun from under the bar at any moment and blow us all away. He said something to us which to this day I've no idea what it was, but Bill and Taffy just replied rather meekly in unison: "Yes please…" assuming he'd asked us if we wanted a beer, which he probably did. Fred and I daren't ask for an orange squash or a Coca-Cola just at that moment, so four glasses of *Lion Beer* were duly plonked onto the bar one after the other with such heavy thumps it seemed as though the barman was determined to smash all the glasses. He then actually pushed them down the bar towards us with his left hand, a distance of several yards, each one sliding along and coming to a stop without a drop being spilt. I felt obliged to drink most of mine, as did Fred, and it tasted reasonably disgusting, or as Fred later very aptly described it as: 'like battery acid'. We didn't say a word to each other, as we noticed *all* the other customers were staring intently at us, also not saying a word. A clock on the wall struck twelve noon, breaking the silence, and I expected Gary Cooper to wander in whistling: *'Oh my darling Clementine'* at any moment. We didn't quite know what to do, and so in true Wild West tradition we each put some change on the bar, probably far too much, and quickly made our exit. As we walked briskly back towards the train my head started spinning from the midday beer on an empty stomach, and we laughed and joked with one another, being careful to glance over our shoulders occasionally in case we were being pursued.

Our next stop, a few hours later, was Mafeking, a very famous place in the British Empire. There was just enough time, while the train took on more water, to have my picture taken next to the station sign. Fred had a brand new Kodak Brownie camera and he was constantly taking snaps with it. Luckily he later gave me some of them; otherwise I wouldn't have any photos from my time in Africa. We managed to buy some supplies too, mainly bread, fruit and soft drinks, from a shop at the station called 'Platform Stores', as we were all starving. We were now on the south eastern edge of the Kalahari Desert, and the afternoon air was becoming very hot and dry. We saw huge numbers of wild animals from the windows of the train, including giraffes, with their peculiar and unlikely manner of running, their long necks nodding awkwardly forwards and back as they ran. I'm sure I also saw lions, and buffalo, and other animals which at the time I was unable to name. It was a magnificent sight and I almost couldn't believe I was really there, seeing all this in the flesh. I will never forget these first incredible sightings I had from the train of the real Africa.

Night fell again on the train, and still none of us had been able to have more than a rudimentary hand and face wash in the tiny sink in the train lavatory, the taps of which only seemed to work intermittently and with a great deal of luck, and we were now sleeping in the same clothes we'd had on since we were on board *The Capetown Castle*. But we still somehow managed to maintain a positive attitude and remained excited about our prospects.

Our second night sleeping in our seats became quite uncomfortable. As we made our way north across the eastern Kalahari it was getting hotter than ever inside the train. But this was nothing compared to the heat in our carriage once the sun came up later the next morning. It was our third day on the train and fourth day in the same clothes, the fabric of which was now sticking to us uncomfortably through layer upon layer of dried and renewed sweat. There were visible tide-marks on our shirts like the irregular foamy lines on Brighton beach. It wasn't just us though, as the carriage was almost full, everyone else was in the same predicament.

People smoked on the train, mainly the foul-smelling local cigarettes, and this combined with the crushing and increasingly pungent smell of so many sweaty bodies made the atmosphere incredibly oppressive. We opened our carriage window as wide as we could in order to allow in some breeze, however warm, and not long after doing so some unknown beast, something truly horrendous, flew into the carriage through the window and flapped around our heads wildly scattering everyone in terror. Amidst much screaming and shouting I dived onto the floor as the monster insect, as that was what it seemed to be, buzzed around up and down the full length of the carriage looking for a victim to set down on. Fred shouted at me and I shouted back and we immediately assumed whatever the thing was that it must have been lethal, a blood-sucking killer, as the other passengers were terror-struck too. Finally, and unluckily for us, it settled on our table, probably sensing the sweet and sticky remains of the pineapple. It then went very quiet, so I plucked up the courage to peer over the edge of the table to get a better look. The creature was a dark brown, evil-looking thing about six inches long, at least. It had long spindly legs with spines on them and I was sure I could see rows of vicious teeth in its jaws.

"Don't touch it, Dennis, it might bite you or sting you or something!" Bill shouted, though I couldn't see him at all. He'd rammed himself, backside first, right under his seat, a feat that any circus contortionist would have been rightly proud of. His head was sticking out and was the only part of him that was visible. I wondered where Taffy was, as I couldn't see him either. I was very envious of him, as he'd obviously found a bloody good hiding place. Not one of us had the courage to swat the thing or at least tackle it in some way, as we just cowered on the floor out of sight.

I'm not sure how long we would have been willing to remain in our hiding places, probably until the giant insect had died of old age. But this wasn't about to happen because just then the door to our carriage was noisily thrown open and an enormous white Afrikaner bloke from the next carriage appeared, no doubt having heard the commotion and decided to investigate. Another followed and the two of them came right up to our table. They laughed at first, but then, seeing us cowering on the floor, one of them shouted in a very thick accent: "You've been very lucky! One touch of those wings on your skin and you're a dead man!"

Bill then whispered to me: "I told you, it's lethal!"

But then the second Afrikaner reached forward and grabbed hold of the insect with one hand and threw it under the table at us shouting: "Pick it up and throw it out of the window, it's only a locust, it's bloody harmless!" and he turned and walked back to his carriage, laughing uncontrollably.

The other began laughing but in a sudden burst of seriousness told us: "If you have your windows open like that, what do you expect? You need to stand guard, particularly in stations, in case a zebra or a lion gets in and gobbles you all up! Sleep tight!" and walked off, following the other, laughing as he walked.

The locust sat quietly in the aisle near our table, preening itself, suddenly looking very innocent. I leaned forward and struck the insect with the back of my right hand and it took off again, heading for the back of the carriage. Someone at the other end opened the door and it flew straight out and safely away into the open. What else could get in the carriage besides that? Should we believe him about the open windows and the possibility of wild animals getting in? We suddenly realised there was more to Africa than we had first thought.

We initially took the advice the Afrikaners had given us and closed all the windows, but it wasn't long before we felt as though we'd suffocate. We opened them again, but perhaps not quite as wide as before. The stench inside the train was just too much to bear with the windows completely closed. And now it seemed the toilet had completely given up and wasn't working at all. It was full of pooh already and now the smell of raw sewage filled the train along with the body odour and stale cigarettes. I opened our nearest window as wide as it would go. I was now sure that the teeth and claws of a wild animal would be much more preferable to the farting, body odour and shit stink of the compartment we were in.

When the sun came up after another very uncomfortable night, the train rolled slowly to a stop, apparently in the middle of nowhere. It had been crawling along by that time anyway, so the fact that it had ceased all forward movement was barely noticeable. It was as though the train had been pulled along by a pair of Blackpool Pleasure Beach donkeys or some trained wildebeest, and now they'd just given up and died on the track. Fred, Bill, Taffy and I were all awake and just stared blankly at one another over the table, mouths open, gasping for air. We sat in saturated silence, utterly soaked in sweat. I swear I could see steam rising from Fred's clothing, and he looked drained and exhausted. None of us had shaved properly for nearly a week and we probably looked like escaped convicts. Then to our astonishment, as the train sat motionless on the track, a pair of dark brown hands appeared at our open window next to us. More hands joined the first pair, the palms of which I noticed were bright pink, and it seemed they were asking us for food. We gave them anything we could spare, biscuits, bread and some fruit, and I noticed these adults then immediately handed what they had to some naked children standing waiting patiently further away from the train. We wished we had more to give, but then the train started easing forwards and we were on our way again. It was day four of our train journey and according to the other passengers we would soon be arriving in Bulawayo.

Our spirits recovered and we took turns in using the sink in the toilet to shave as best we could, using Taffy's razor which he'd luckily kept with him in his pocket, and generally tidy ourselves up. The view from our window became quite amazing again, as we saw more wild animals wandering around the vast landscape. This included the usual giraffe, elephants and wildebeest, but where we passed rivers and waterholes we also saw hippos. We had now passed into Southern Rhodesia and we soon arrived in Bulawayo. We all alighted from the train, very happy to be getting off at last, took our luggage, and walked together into the station. We were met by none other than the seemingly ubiquitous John Brandt, complete with renewed sun tan, and who seemed extremely pleased to see us. He was warm and friendly as usual, and gave us some fantastic news, informing us that we would be given a room in a nearby hotel for the day where we could relax and freshen up. Clearly the train journey we'd just experienced was renowned for the lack of comfort, so a few hours in a nice hotel was extremely welcome. We arranged to meet John in the lobby of the hotel later, and Fred and I headed upstairs to our room. I sank into a deep hot bath and days of sweat and grime formed a greasy brown layer on the surface of my bath water. My underwear was beyond recovery, as it was thickly stained due to some rather loose bowel problems in the previous few days. They looked as though they should have been disposed of with a flame-thrower, rather than washed. I threw them away; as I did the socks I'd been wearing.

The four of us sat in the hotel restaurant feeling wonderful and refreshed, and were joined by John Brandt. He spoke enthusiastically about what was to come, and laughed uproariously when we told him of the escapade with the locust on the train. I mentioned the Africans reaching in the train for food, but he seemed disinterested and changed the subject. We ate a fantastic meal of steak, and then more steak, with so much chewing involved that our jaws ached. But it was a fantastic meal; all washed down with glasses of wonderful chilled 'Oros', South African orange squash.

After six hours in the hotel and as the sun set, we returned to the station for the final onward leg of the journey. John shook our hands in turn and wished us all good luck. We had to endure just one more night on the train, but this time feeling fresh and rested. At around midnight we passed through a small town called Wankie, before apparently passing Victoria Falls, though of course in the total darkness we didn't see any of it. The train stopped for a while in Livingstone, which seemed to be a popular destination as quite a few passengers left the train and also boarded. We were close enough to hear the distant rumble of the falls, a strange and eerie sound at night. We had to wait for over an hour for the train to complete its 'bunkering', which is picking up fresh coal and water for the engine, before we resumed our journey.

A couple of hours later the train stopped again in another small town called Choma. We were now in Northern Rhodesia, and sadly this was where we said goodbye to Bill and Taffy. I was sorry to see them go, but this was where they were due to work. They were great fellows and I was a little upset at leaving them there on the platform at Choma. Fred and I then slept for several hours before the train smoothly rolled to a stop in Lusaka station. We jumped down onto the station platform to stretch our legs. We were now very close to our final destination, Broken Hill. The sun came up and I began to feel incredibly excited.

ARRIVAL: BROKEN HILL

It was late in the morning of the fifth day when we arrived at the small town in the middle of the bush known as Broken Hill. It was a beautiful day, clear and cloudless; a perfect late spring morning in Africa. Even after all these years I remember my arrival in Broken Hill vividly, as though it was only yesterday. I felt utterly euphoric, as though I was in some abstract summer dream, and I'd wake up at any moment back in the darkened gloom of Sheffield in the depth of a freezing winter.

Fred and I were met and escorted by a chirpy little chap from head office on foot, a few hundred yards towards where we would be living. As we left the station I realised why the train had struggled at times on our journey from the Cape. The station name had a few very interesting figures underneath it: '*Altitude 3,870 feet.*' It seemed we'd climbed as high as a small mountain in the last few days. I then turned briefly towards the sound of shrieking and laughing from further down the track. I saw a train standing near the station with half a dozen open goods wagons full of native Africans, jumping around wildly, giggling and laughing as two white men were soaking them all with a hose.

Our escort stopped in front of a single-storey building surrounded by a neatly mown lawn, with white-washed walls and corrugated iron roof, which he euphemistically called our 'bungalow'. He handed us a key each after unlocking the door with one of them. We had a brief tour of the interior before he said:

"That's it, gentlemen. Make yourselves at home and enjoy your stay. You will each have a boy, a servant, and they should be round to see you before sundown. So, good luck to you both".

He walked out the door and was gone. In no great haste

Fred and I decided on which room to take before inspecting our accommodation. The bungalow was actually more than adequate, with two en-suite bedrooms, a fully equipped communal kitchen, and comfortable living area. It was clean and tidy, and contained everything we would need, including an old record player with one LP, Tchaikovsky's '5th Symphony'. Each room was light and spacious, but because the place had obviously been closed up for a while we opened all the windows as wide as we could to let some air in. A fine white net hung from the ceiling over each bed. So this was it, my home for the next two years! Fred and I congratulated one another and shook hands in celebration before unpacking our things.

Late in the afternoon there was some tapping on the front door of the bungalow and a young black lad, probably in his late teens, walked in. He came up to me showing off some beautiful white teeth in a very broad smile:

"*Bwana,* me John," he said, and continued rattling away, speaking so fast in broken English that I could hardly understand what he was saying. I managed to hear the words 'laundry', 'sweeping' and 'washing' and I took this to mean that he would be doing almost all these chores for me. This was an extraordinary new experience for me, to have a personal servant, one who was not my mother I mean! A few minutes later another black lad tapped on the door and walked in. He introduced himself to Fred in much the same way, and he called himself Bert. John and Bert seemed to know exactly what to do as they went straight into our belongings, removed the dirty washing and then left. Soon after this, and just as the light started fading quickly in a rapid twilight, someone else knocked on our front door. I opened it and saw a tall, handsome, fair-haired white man who smiled at me briefly then strode confidently straight in:

"Hello chaps, I'm Richard, Richard Baines, I live in the next bungalow along from you, I saw you arrive earlier, pleased to meet you." A brown briar pipe was balancing in one corner of his mouth gripped tightly in his teeth, though it wasn't lit, and he took it out and held it between the forefinger and thumb of his left hand while he shook our hands in turn quite vigorously.

"Great to see you chaps, welcome aboard! Welcome to Africa by the way. Just off the boat from dear old Blighty are you? Jolly well done. A bit different over here, eh? They're nice chaps though, the natives I mean, if you don't upset 'em!"

I wasn't sure whether he meant the native black people or the other white residents, but he carried on:

"I'm being transferred to Salisbury next week, but I'd still like to get to know you chaps, we're a close knit lot on the railways you know, and you never know when you might want to catch the old transfer train!"

We sat down in the living area and Fred and I introduced ourselves. Richard fumbled about in a pocket of his khaki shorts and pulled out a bulging black leather fold-over pouch. He opened it and began loading some dark brown stringy bits of tobacco into his pipe, pressing it down tightly with his right thumb. He then lit it with a match and after some audible gurgling and sucking noises great clouds of white, sweet smelling smoke began to cover him completely. In between numerous rapid little puffs, creating ever more smoke which then started to fill the room, he went on to tell us that we'd need someone to show us around, and he kindly volunteered to do this the next day. His demeanour reminded me of the conman, Digby Caruthers, though he wasn't quite so pompous.

After a few minutes Richard suddenly stood up: "Good heavens can't have this you know, too risky out here..." and moved quickly to the nearest window. He reached for the handles and drew them together, shutting it completely. "Mozzies, you know, out here. Hasn't anyone told you, there's malaria in these parts. Can't be too careful. There's some other things too, little nasties, but you'll no doubt meet them yourselves!"

He then went from room to room closing all the windows in the bungalow, leaving a thick smoke trail as he did so, which whirled and spiralled after him in his wake. When he'd finished he came over to us and stood still for a few moments, drawing on his pipe, apparently deep in thought before announcing: "I'm so sorry. You must be exhausted. I'll call around in the morning; shall we say eight-thirty? See you tomorrow then, bye for now!" And promptly left. Our bungalow was now sealed tight and looked as though someone had just thrown a smoke grenade through the door.

I slept soundly in my bed that night, despite the air being thick with the smell of Richard's pipe smoke. It was my first night in a bed for almost a week and my first ever night sleeping under a mosquito net. I didn't see any mosquitos or flies of any sort, at least not that night, but I suppose they were there, hence the reason for the net, unless they'd all died of pipe smoke inhalation. In the morning Richard kept his promise and was at our door promptly at eight-thirty. He was lively and convivial, and walked us to the administration offices, which were smarter and more modern than I had imagined. He introduced Fred to the accounts manager, and it seemed Fred would be replacing Richard in the accounts office. I was then introduced to the head of the Rhodesia Railways commercial branch, a chap called Sonny Amyot, a dark haired, olive-skinned white man of French descent. He was quick to say he was a Huguenot, but a South African citizen with strong links to Britain. He showed me a large Union Jack which he always kept under his desk, though I've no idea why. To my initial disappointment I was told I would be posted to the commercial division and not the train operating division. But Mr Amyot stated it would be interesting work, and the office needed new blood with fresh ideas. I was shown my desk, which was directly opposite his, and he shook my hand with a warm smile saying:

"Welcome to Rhodesia Railways!"

Fred and I had the rest of the day to ourselves. We wandered around exploring our new home. We found a wonderful, huge open-air swimming pool which we were both very excited about, and came across a clubhouse with a bar, which due to some strange local by-laws was only open for two hours a day, between five o'clock and seven o'clock. This was The Broken Hill Railway Recreation Club, and we were to be full members automatically. We decided to return later to see what it was like. Maybe there was a pool table, or a snooker room or some other similar facilities. We made our way back to our bungalow and both wrote some letters home, telling of our safe arrival. My new servant, John, came in, carrying my laundry: a cleaned and pressed shirt and a pair of trousers I'd worn on the train, beautifully clean and ironed. I was very impressed. He washed some pots in the sink then left. Fred and I dozed for a while in the afternoon heat and found a small round radio in the living room. We tuned it in to a station called *Radio Brazzaville*, broadcast from somewhere over the border in the Congo. There were very few stations but this played the sort of music Fred and I quite liked.

We made our way back to the club bar at five o'clock. Once inside we found the only facility was the bar itself. No pool table or snooker room, just the bar, with drinking being the main pastime. The club filled up rapidly with fellow white railway workers, British men mainly, with some white Afrikaners, who started drinking immediately and very quickly. Some appeared to drink as though it was their last day on earth. At that rate it probably would be. I ordered a glass of Oros orange juice, and Fred drank a glass of Coca-Cola. This became our drinking routine, the two of us either drinking Coke or Oros, and never beer or spirits.

Within half an hour the place was in chaos and most people were successfully getting themselves as drunk as they possibly could in as short a time as possible. So-called 'binge drinking' is said to be a modern British phenomenon, but these drinkers in this bar could have out-drunk anyone around today. I would guess the restricted opening hours didn't help, and the fact that booze was seemingly unavailable anywhere else. There was no corner shop, off-licence, or supermarket to visit. I sat with a tall, very conspicuous glass of Oros juice, quite bemused by what was happening. I was just about to suggest to Fred that we leave when a very drunken chap with a whiskey in one hand and a large cigar in the other wandered over and sat next to me, close up, as though we were the best of friends.

"Need a barman. You're new here aren't you? Interested? We'll pay you of course. What do you think?" He looked at me, or rather through me, as he was so drunk his eyes were completely glazed over. I don't think he even noticed Fred.

"Well, I'd not given it any thought, until you just asked…" I replied, trying to be pleasant, baffled by the immediacy of the offer.

Cigar smoke and whiskey breath completely enveloped me like a poisonous cloud, and he then said, or rather ordered me in a more than slightly peremptory tone: "Come and see me tomorrow after lunch in my office, there, look, there…" and he pointed to a door at the end of the bar, "and we'll discuss it, right?" and promptly stood up, swaying, and moved away, walking with deliberate wide steps as though on board a ship in a high sea. Either that or he'd just shit himself.

Fred laughed, and looking astonished at me said: "Who on earth was that?" and we both laughed, watching the man wobble across the room and up to a group of other men standing in a thick fog of tobacco smoke. The bar was five deep and I noticed our neighbour, Richard, was leaning against it at an impossible angle, deep in conversation with a couple of men, all talking loudly at one another. There were two young white lads behind the bar, clearly extremely busy.

Fred and I left and made our way back to the bungalow. As we walked we heard some very deep men's voices chanting and singing in unison somewhere ahead of us. The singing echoed from the corners of the buildings all around and seemed to fill the air. It was quite melodious and in a language I'd not heard before. As we rounded a corner we almost collided with a pair of black men, each carrying two large buckets suspended on the end of a pole resting across their shoulders. They passed us, singing continuously, and as they did so the smell of what they were carrying hit us like a wave of poisonous gas. It seemed they were carrying large buckets of shit which sloshed and slopped around in the heavy containers. They didn't say anything to us but carried on walking and singing, heading out of Broken Hill. We later found out these were part of a team of such men nick-named *the Black Watch.* Working in three pairs it was their job to carry away the excrement from some of the toilets, dumping it all nearby in a place known colloquially as 'Crap Canyon', situated in 'Crap Alley'.

I then realised as I walked down the track from the club that I didn't get the drunken chap's name who'd offered me the job in the bar. I guessed that he might have forgotten about it the next day anyway.

THE NEW JOB

My first full day at work in the office started very slowly. Initially I had nothing to do and felt quite self-conscious about it. But then someone handed me several thick, leather-bound ledger books and some invoices, a stack of receipts, payment slips and lists of train times with freight movements, and soon I was very busy. Rhodesia Railways transported huge amounts of freight across that part of Africa, mainly minerals and raw materials, amounting to millions of tons a year, so this was all very lucrative for the company. There was a mine in Broken Hill, right on our doorstep, producing lead, zinc, and even silver, all of which needed transportation. The roads were little more than dirt tracks, so virtually everything went by rail. I had to make sure the company was paid correctly and on time for its services to the mining industry, and I soon found out that business was booming. I had to submit estimates to the mining companies of how much it would cost them for us to move their materials on our railways, and some of the figures and tonnage was simply staggering. We were moving an average of 1600 tons of copper slab *every day* from the copper mining area, a vast region known as the Copper Belt. Africa was being stripped of its resources on a massive scale. I became familiar with place names such as Chingola, Kitwe, Ndola, and there was even a huge mine at Wankie, the town we'd passed near Victoria Falls.

Just after lunch I remembered the appointment at the club made by the drunk the night before. Even though I wasn't sure it was genuine I walked down there to see if I was expected. I didn't even know the man's name, and I was sure he didn't know mine. The front door of the club was well and truly locked, but before I returned to work I thought I'd see if there was a back way in. Sure enough I pushed gently against a door leading into a storage area where I saw crates of whiskey, gin, brandy and barrels of beer, all stacked halfway up to the ceiling. I was spotted almost immediately by a young black lad rolling a beer barrel rather clumsily along the corridor, and who seemed to be expecting me, as he just said: "*Bwana,* come, *bwana…*" and abandoning the barrel he led me to the office. The same chap was in the office who I'd spoken to the night before.

"Come in young man, sit yourself down…" he pointed to a chair in front of his enormous desk. I immediately detected a slur in his speech which I dismissed at first, not thinking he could possibly have been drinking so early in the day, and when the bar was not yet open. He was probably middle-aged and was quite overweight, with a pencil moustache and a thick head of dark hair, or at least from the position in my chair at that moment it looked like thick hair. He had sharp angular features and a long face, and was very pale considering he'd been in Africa for some time.

"You don't drink do you?" he asked, in an almost disbelieving, accusatory manner.

"No, I don't. Never have," I replied, aware that though he was probably not a tall man he seemed to be sitting very upright and somehow much higher in his seat than me.

"Well, we need someone with a clear head, you know. Done any bar work, have you, do you think you can do it?" as he fixed a stare at me, pursing his lips then rubbing his chin with his right hand.

"Yes, I think so, I mean I haven't done any bar work before but I think I can do it, of course, why not?" I replied, realising as he looked across his desk at me that he was either drunk or in the first stages of having a stroke.

"Then the job's yours…" he said, just as he slowly closed his eyes and started sliding very smoothly sideways off his chair. He parted company with it and collapsed in an undignified heap on the floor next to his desk with an enormous thump, like a large sack of King Edwards potatoes. He was followed immediately by an avalanche of cushions which sprang off his chair and then partially buried him and obscured his face. He didn't move or say anything. I didn't know what to do and thought he'd died, so I jumped up and pulled the cushions away. At first it seemed as though he'd seriously and fatally cracked his head wide open until I realised his hair had flipped off his head in one great, matted comb-over which then lay neatly alongside him on the floor. He suddenly started snoring loudly, like a walrus stranded on a beach, so with some relief I realised he was obviously still alive. I stared at him for a moment before rising to my feet. *That would appear to be the end of the interview*, I thought to myself as I walked out of the office.

Within a few days of our arrival at Broken Hill, in early December, we were treated to some of the most spectacular displays of lightning and the most tremendous thunderstorms, the likes of which I'd never seen before. The 'rainy season' apparently started in late October or early November, so it seemed it was late. I was at work at my desk in mid-afternoon when the first storm struck Broken Hill. The clap of thunder came as such a shock and was so loud I jumped off my chair and went to hide under my desk, much to the amusement of my colleagues in the office. It sounded so very much like the German bombs dropped on Sheffield in the Blitz, complete with the shaking of the earth and rattling windows. Once I'd explained this to Sonny and the others they seemed to understand why I'd leapt under my desk like a frightened rabbit.

The rain fell so heavily and so quickly the dirt roads were instantly turned into fast flowing torrents, completely indistinguishable as roads. The street lights that lined the few roads that had them looked odd and incongruous, utterly pointless in what had now become impassable, muddy rivers. Lightning danced across the sky in wonderful purple and white patterns against the huge blue-black clouds and was visible from many miles away. It was possible to count ten or fifteen seconds before the sound of the thunder eventually reached us. In between the storms it was still hot and sunny; indeed, even when it rained it was hot by British standards. Huge flying ants an inch long emerged in their thousands in the moist atmosphere and the local Africans collected them in large containers to dry them out and eat later. Once the wings had been removed they looked, and probably tasted, much like very small prawns, and were no doubt full of protein. These ants were not to be confused with the venomous black Matebele ants, which Fred and I discovered if crushed under foot would issue a particularly foul smell, to the extent they were nicknamed the 'gas ants'.

Both Fred and I became heavily involved in our work and were understandably keen to make a good impression. Our neighbour, Richard, left for Salisbury and his house was empty for a few days until an English married couple, Janet and Colin, moved in. They were very quiet and tended to socialise with other couples in Broken Hill, so I didn't get to know them particularly well. Two weeks after I arrived I was sent down to Bulawayo for a two-day training course on 'Refunds & Claims'. It was great to have a short break from the routine but when I returned it was nice to be back in the increasingly familiar surroundings of Broken Hill.

I was beginning to understand more about the nature of where I was living and developed an increasing curiosity for it. I discovered the town had been named in the early 20th century after a similar mining town of the same name in New South Wales, Australia, and I occasionally imagined what this other twin town would look like. Back at my desk I could now calculate ticket refunds between destinations, sometimes over long distances and involving complex calculations. There was also a certain amount of 'sheet slashing' of the freight wagons, usually at night by the Africans who would climb onto the trains and rip open the covering sheets, pulling out anything they could and throwing the items down to the ground.

While I was in Bulawayo I managed to buy some materials for kite making, bundles of bamboo cane, sheets of paper and string, ready for the end of the rainy season and hopefully some kite flying. Meanwhile Fred and I had managed to acquire a pedal cycle each and in between the showers and thunderstorms we began exploring the countryside around Broken Hill. Our adventures were modest at first, daring only to travel five or ten miles into the bush on some very difficult muddy tracks. But we were thoroughly enjoying our time and began to feel like real explorers.

On one of our early cycling trips we encountered elephants at close quarters for the first time. I remember it was a very quiet Saturday afternoon and we'd cycled for miles into open bush land on an often arduous and remote track, and had not seen another human being for several hours. We decided to stop and take a drink from our water bag, which was slung over my back. The trees and bushes were quite dense where we'd stopped and we sat down by the path to rest for a while. I first heard a thudding sound, like heavy footsteps some distance behind us through the trees, accompanied by what sounded like someone, or something, ripping a tree apart, with a loud tearing and cracking of branches. The noise seemed to move around and past us through the trees and then ahead of us. There was no other sound of any sort, nothing to indicate what it was, but whatever it was, it was clearly getting closer.

Fred and I looked at one another and picked up our bikes. We didn't know what to do and we both suddenly felt very exposed and vulnerable. Then only fifty yards in front of us they emerged and walked slowly across the track. There were five fully grown, huge beasts, and one calf the size of a small donkey. We were close enough to them to hear the gentle flapping of their ears against their sides and we could see the deep ridges in their skin, ingrained with mud. The biggest of them saw us and raised his trunk and gave out a huge trumpet roar, probably to warn us off, which it certainly did! I felt hugely privileged to be so close to such magnificent wild animals and looked on in a state of near disbelief. They eventually ambled away from us, paying us little attention, leaving Fred and I speechless and fired up for more such encounters.

On our return to Broken Hill, we were keen to tell everyone who would listen to us about what we'd seen, but instead of being lauded with praise for being brave explorers we were warned the elephants should not have been there, and neither should we! We'd ventured into the bush miles from anywhere with not a single rifle between us. Fred and I were distraught, and from then on we didn't discuss our cycling trips into the bush.

The Christmas and New Year celebrations at Broken Hill were unlike anything I'd experienced before. I know it's traditional to be merry over the festive period but most people seemed to be drunk almost constantly for two weeks. I was drafted in to work behind the bar on some nights and couldn't believe the levels of intoxication some people could reach, and yet still manage to hold a conversation and even walk out of the club unaided at closing time. Day after day without a break the same people would drink themselves into oblivion, returning for more of the same each night. I couldn't understand how some of them remained alive in such conditions.

It also seemed very strange to be in such a warm climate at the end of December, when I knew that back home there would most likely be snow, ice, and sub-zero temperatures daily.

THE POLICE RESERVE

Soon after our arrival in Broken Hill, Fred and I were conscripted into the local police, as part-time reservists. All newcomers had to do this, and it was apparently in our contract, though I don't remember seeing it! We were informed only a few days after our arrival that we would be called up, but it didn't actually happen until the festive season was well and truly over. There was a police station near our offices and we were duly summoned there together one Saturday morning early in January 1951.

The police station in Broken Hill was a dreary, forbidding building, both inside and out. The interior could best be described as Spartan and austere, with a uniquely pungent odour that was a mixture of vomit, sweat, stale cigarettes and carbolic soap. To be blunt, it was a dark and shabby place that was so unwelcoming as to be downright intimidating. Perhaps this was the intention. It was staffed mainly by loud, aggressive and thoroughly unpleasant white Afrikaner men who were incredibly arrogant and rude. We were firstly escorted into a dreary office where we signed some papers and provided our details. We were then asked about any previous experience, particularly with firearms. We'd both endured National Service quite recently so this seemed to be met with some modest approval by the sergeant in charge.

We were ushered through a series of heavy locked doors and into the open air in the back yard of the station. It was a huge open space of untidy scrubland with a high wall all around, which must have been at least a hundred yards to the far end. We were each handed a rifle, which I recognised as a British Lee Enfield .303, given a magazine of bullets, and told to aim at the targets hanging in front of a huge pile of sand at the far wall. Shooting was one of the very few past times I'd enjoyed in the army, probably because I was quite good at it.

We both lay down on the ground and took aim. Most of my first shots hit the target, but Fred missed his completely, with sand far from his target flying wildly into the air after every shot. I did a little better in the next round but Fred continued to miss and was subjected to a tirade of highly personal verbal abuse from several Afrikaners, only some of which I could understand.

"You couldn't hit a barn door!" I whispered to Fred in between shots.

"I could hit you with it from here if you're not careful!" he replied, clearly exasperated at why none of his shots seemed to be going anywhere he wanted. I felt quite smug and was enjoying the exercise, until we were each then handed a loaded revolver, a shiny black Webley pistol, and told to try shooting at some targets fifty yards in front of us. To my horror I missed each time and so did Fred. I'd never fired a pistol before and suddenly all my shooting confidence drained away in an instant. Fred said he couldn't get used to the sights and the recoil on the rifle, and now I had the same problem with the pistol. To me it just seemed incredibly loud, unpredictable and inaccurate. There's no doubt that if there'd been a barn door to shoot at I'd have missed it every time! Two Afrikaners then calmly wandered into the firing area and fixed a black paper circle about twelve inches across to a post no more than twenty-five yards in front of us. While we waited I noticed some dark clouds gathering high above us threatening another storm. We were each then handed a rifle again and told to fire once on command of: 'Fire!' at the target. This time we both hit it dead centre, probably because it was so close. I shuddered when I realised this was firing squad training.

We had no more training of any sort, firearms or otherwise, and as the weeks passed we both forgot about it. Then one night in early February I was told to report to the police station at seven-thirty the following morning. I was concerned about my job but was told I would be excused for a day in order to fulfil my policing obligations. I was also concerned because Fred had not been asked to go, nor it would seem had anyone else. I arrived at the police station on time, more than a little nervous, and walked in. It was still the rainy season, though it was now in decline, and I took suitable clothing with me. The sergeant pulled out a rather tatty map of the local area from a drawer and spread it over his desk.

"You see this village here?" he said in a very strong Afrikaans accent. He reached for a pencil and drew a cross over a small settlement which appeared to be about three miles from Broken Hill.

"The monkeys are brewing again! Go and sort the blick bastards out!" and he prodded the cross on the map with the index finger of his right hand over and over, looking at me angrily, as though whatever was happening was my fault.

Another uniformed policeman said: "Yeah that's right, put a stop to it, do your duty, man," but I still didn't know what I had to do. I must have looked a little confused because the sergeant then said: "They've got themselves an illegal still again, and they've been making spirits. Get rid of it and sort them out!"

I was handed a Police Reserve armband and rolled it up my left sleeve. I couldn't believe I was about to be sent on my own to sort out an unruly village possibly full of drunken natives. I picked up the map and tried to work out how I could get to the village. As I walked toward the door the sergeant shouted me back.

"Here, take this, and use it if you have to!" and he passed me a loaded Webley pistol. I didn't have a holster for it so after quickly checking the safety catch was on I pushed it barrel first into the waistband of my shorts, then covered it over with my shirt. I was acutely aware the end of the barrel was pointing directly at my family jewels, but I had no other way of carrying it. I stepped out into the street and orientated the map in the direction I needed to go. A hundred yards down the street I joined a track which was little more than a footpath and headed off into the bush. According to the shabby and stained police map this should take me straight to the village.

The further I went from Broken Hill the denser the trees

and bushes became. I felt as though I was being watched all the time, not by human beings but by the wild animals. I took out the pistol and held it in my right hand. I flicked the safety catch off; I was aware that if anything attacked me that was smaller than a barn door I'd have no chance hitting it. Fifteen anxious minutes passed and I came to a fork in the path. *Do I go left or right?* The map didn't even show this at all, so I had to guess. I took the path to the right and after another ten minutes found myself heading back towards the town. I hurriedly retraced my steps and took the left fork. I wondered what I was going to find when I reached the village. Was I supposed to arrest them all and march them back to the station? What if they wanted to fight me? Was I expected to shoot one of them, or all of them? What if I *did* shoot one of them? What if they were all drunk and unconscious? Suddenly I didn't want to be there. For the first time since I'd left England I just wanted to be home. I wished I'd never left. I wished I was back in Sheffield in the freezing February cold, wandering around the Sheaf Market with modest ambitions and minding my own business, and not out there in Africa stupidly pretending to be something I very definitely wasn't!

I heard movement in the undergrowth around me and my imagination was making the situation far worse. I thought I saw a lion, but a second look proved me wrong, it was just a fallen tree. I then saw a huge monkey, a baboon, which seemed to be laughing and pointing at me. After almost an hour of walking I'd become a complete nervous wreck, shaking and sweating not just from the increasing early morning heat but from the fearful anticipation of what was ahead. I couldn't believe that if necessary I had authority to shoot at and possibly kill another human being. This was just so far above my comprehension that I very nearly threw the gun into the bush and ran back to my bungalow.

Quite suddenly I walked into a clearing and saw several large round huts each with neatly thatched roofs. I retreated and stood for a moment hiding ridiculously behind a small avocado tree. I could feel my heart pounding and I realised I was sweating and shaking. I'd heard stories that the natives could successfully impale a baboon with a spear from a hundred yards away, and that they could run as fast as a cheetah. I had terrible visions of being overpowered and thrown into some huge cooking pot and boiled alive. I remember thinking quite bizarrely that I would probably not taste very nice.

I couldn't see anyone around so I decided to make my move, and to try each hut in turn. I walked into the first and luckily found what I'd been sent there for. In front of me was a Heath Robinson contraption of metal containers and buckets with pipes everywhere which looked remarkably as though it could be a still. I put my gun back into my belt, not wanting to antagonise anyone unnecessarily. Just then a very tall, thin black man, probably in his thirties, walked into the hut, followed by some small children. The youngsters seemed to defuse the tension slightly but for a moment I didn't know what to do. Much to my relief I wasn't grabbed or attacked in any way. We just stood rigid, staring at one another for a moment. I felt I needed to finish what I'd started so I stepped forward and kicked the bottom half of the still, causing the rest of it to collapse in a noisy cacophony of metallic rattling and banging. I looked at the man and said: "No good, no good!" pointing at the remnants of the still on the ground.

He reached down and picked up a tin cup containing a clear liquid and very politely offered it to me:

"Bwana, bwana!"

I took it from him and sure enough, it smelt like cheap gin or vodka, so I threw it into the pile of wreckage, repeating: "No, no good, no good!" I looked at him and said: "Police, police," and pointed in the direction of Broken Hill. I stepped out the hut and he followed. I indicated for him to come with me, which to my amazement he seemed happy to do. I started walking with him towards Broken Hill. I then realised I'd made my first arrest.

My prisoner, who I referred to as 'boss man' led the way back through the bush and was an excellent guide. I'm not saying he found short cuts but we seemed to be within sight of the town a good deal sooner than on my outward journey. I began to wonder what sort of reception this chap would get when we arrived at the police station. I feared he would not be treated particularly well to say the least, and I didn't want to be responsible for this. As we drew closer to the town I stopped us both and pointed back towards the village.

"Go, you go back!" I shouted at him, and he immediately understood what I meant. He turned and disappeared into the bush. I rehearsed what I was going to say to the sergeant a hundred times. I needed to show confidence and a degree of pretend arrogance in order to convince him I'd achieved what was expected of me. When I arrived at the police station I strode into the building with a swagger, ready for my inquisitor, only to find another sergeant behind the desk. I told him I'd found and destroyed the still and had thoroughly dealt with the miscreants responsible, though I wasn't specific in what I'd done. The new sergeant couldn't have seemed less concerned and didn't even ask me about it. I suddenly felt deflated but also pleased and relieved. There was no paperwork to complete, nowhere to record what I'd done, and seemingly no accountability whatsoever. I handed over the map and the revolver and told them I'd not fired a shot. Again, none of them seemed bothered. I could have killed half the village and it seemed they weren't interested. I handed back my armband and returned to the bungalow, very glad and relieved the ordeal was over.

That night the events of the day and my first police work went through my mind a dozen times. It was the careless attitude in the police station that struck me the most, and the sheer unprofessional manner and unaccountability of the officers. I became wary of getting tangled up with them and stayed clear as much as I could. I told Fred what had happened and about the atmosphere in the police station, but he just shrugged and said: "None of our business".

He changed his mind a few weeks later when it was his turn to be an armband cop for a day. He described an incident to me that happened in the afternoon of the day he was on duty.

It was a particularly hot day and one of the first really dry days after the rainy season. Quite unannounced a young, well-built black African man walked in through the front door of the police station carrying a dirty and stained canvas bag. He was shaking and visibly upset, according to Fred, and with tears streaming down his face he walked straight past him and up to the sergeant in charge. He was cursing in his native language, either Shona or IsiNdebele, and dropped the heavy bag on the desk. He continued talking at the sergeant as though asking him questions in a desperately pleading and accusatory manner. The sergeant stood up and indicated for Fred and the other constables present to get hold of the man. Just before he was restrained he tipped the contents of the bag onto the table. It was a woman's severed head. The man was dragged into the back of the station, along with the contents of his bag, which it later became evident was his wife. Fred was excluded from the next events but he says what he saw and heard he never wanted to witness again. He gained the impression the man was blaming the police for what had happened to his wife. It must have taken a huge amount of personal courage for him to walk into the police station the way he did.

Fred was very quiet and not his usual self for days afterwards. Today it would have been said that he'd been traumatised by the experience. We sat on the front steps of our bungalow and watched the gorgeous sunset and the stars appear one by one in the wide African sky, as though they were being turned on one at a time by God himself. It seemed the paradise we'd found wasn't quite such a paradise after all.

"MAL MAL!"

The rains gradually came to an end in March. We were issued with an insect spray to use in our bungalow, and warned to use it regularly, particularly last thing at night due to the high risk of malaria. It was probably DDT or a derivative, but it was colourless and odourless. Each night we sprayed around the bungalow and under the beds, more in a perfunctory manner than with any serious intent. We had no idea just how real the malaria threat was. I'd had a few mosquitos trapped inside the net with me and it was strange how they always seemed to go straight for the ears, so you would immediately hear the tell-tale high pitch buzzing that would announce their presence. It was impossible to sleep while the damnable insect was still alive in the net with you, so it had to be caught and destroyed at all costs. On one occasion I was leaping around on my bed like an idiot, stark naked trying to kill a particularly elusive little bastard with a fly swatter when I lost my balance and fell through the net. Of course I instinctively grabbed at anything I could as I fell and ripped the whole net down and ended up in a naked netted heap on the floor. I assumed I'd probably been bitten but had not contracted any diseases, so I presumed the threat had been exaggerated. I was very much mistaken.

One particularly lovely morning in April 1951, I was up out of my bed as usual at seven o'clock and padded into the kitchen in my bare feet to make the usual breakfast of tea, toast and fried eggs. It was a fine sunny morning at the end of the rainy season, and it was obvious we were about to experience clear blue skies and sunshine all day. Fred and I would often take turns to cook in the morning, and that particular day the pleasure was mine. I flung the windows wide open and the fresh sweet-smelling African morning flooded into the bungalow and mixed with the pungent smells of my breakfast cooking, creating a fantastic and familiar atmosphere. I turned on the wireless and began whistling a tune first to myself and then out loud, and stomped heavily around the kitchen on the wooden floor, which was usually enough to rouse my housemate. But on this particular morning he seemed to be sleeping in longer than usual. When the tea was made I shouted towards Fred's door:

"Come on you lazy Lancastrian, get up!" and I poured two cups, mine with two generous spoons of sugar. I sat at the kitchen table waiting for him to emerge. Curiously there was no sound from his room at all, no movement or noise of any kind. I took more slurps of my tea and noticed the eggs were just about done. The smell alone was usually enough to get him up. I left my tea at the table and walked over towards his room. I opened his door and walked in. Fred was lying on his back on his bed looking perfectly normal, but as I stepped up closer to him I noticed he was utterly drenched in sweat; in fact the whole bed was soaked as though someone had thrown a bucket of water over him. It was then that I noticed his entire body was trembling as though he'd just been pulled from a frozen lake. I shouted his name but there was no response. There were signs that he'd been sick in the night, as dried puke was caked into the sheets next to him and smudged across parts of his face. I shouted him again and took hold of his right shoulder and shook him, in a vain attempt to rouse him. Nothing seemed to work and I was struck by a sudden rush of fear and panic.

My first instinct was to tell someone, anyone, and try to get help. I immediately ran next door and informed Janet and Colin. Judging by the state I was in and how worried I must have looked, when I told him Fred's symptoms Colin didn't bother coming into our bungalow but rushed up towards the office shouting back that he was going to ring for an ambulance. I didn't click at first as to what it could be; I just knew it was obviously very serious. I returned to sit with Fred and was joined by Janet, but we had no idea what to do. Within ten minutes and with a huge sense of relief a large and very sleek white ambulance with some wide red crosses on all sides arrived to take Fred to the mine hospital. The two smartly dressed ambulance men said very little, other than: "You can come and see him later, right?" before sliding him into the back of the vehicle and speeding away.

Our 'boys' John and Bert turned up as usual at eight o'clock and when I told them what had happened they both shouted in unison: "Mal mal! Mal mal!" so I then guessed that it was malaria.

When I arrived at work an hour later, few people seemed surprised to hear about Fred's condition, in fact it seemed to be almost part of a routine. I was given leave from work to pay him a visit, and I arrived at the mine hospital at eleven-thirty that morning. Fred was in a ward of nine other beds, all occupied by white men most of who were moaning and groaning, obviously in some discomfort. Fred was still asleep, so I spoke to the grey-haired Afrikaans doctor and asked him about his condition.

"It could take a week or so, but he should make a full recovery. You live in the same bungalow, is that right?" he looked at me accusingly and I wondered why he was asking me this question.

"Yes, I do, why?"

"You should really get yourself tested you know. If you haven't got it, then we'd like to use some of your blood. Do you know what blood group you are?"

"AB negative," I said, knowing it was very rare.

"Even better!" he said with enthusiasm, "Come along, that is, if you don't mind?" and he gently but firmly took my right arm and led me into a small surgery where he sat me on a chair next to a small bed. He immediately began opening a clear sterile packet with a syringe and needle inside. Before I could really voice any serious objections he'd taken a sample of blood from my right arm, and sealed the tiny bottle, marking a label on the side quickly and deftly with a single squiggle from his pen.

"Can you come back later, say about five o'clock, and we'll have a result for you?"

"Yes, fine," I said, and just as I turned to leave he said:

"Don't worry about your friend, he'll be fine. It's just a touch of malaria."

I returned to work but my mind was preoccupied with thoughts of Fred. 'A touch of malaria?' I wondered how it was possible merely to have a small amount of such a dangerous illness. I was unprepared should anything happen to Fred if he had to return to England, or worse. But the fortunes of the day were later rescued when I made a fantastic discovery. I found out that as we worked for the railway we were entitled to join the 'Car Club' and make use of a car occasionally if we wanted to. I immediately thought of our adventures into the bush and how much further we'd then be able to go. We'd heard of a brilliant place about thirty miles from Broken Hill called Mulungushi Dam, which we had been planning to visit on our bikes. If we had a car, then there would be no limit to how far we could go, and the amount of provisions we could take!

I was desperate to tell Fred this good news, and five o'clock couldn't come around quick enough when I returned to the hospital. To my great relief this time Fred was not only conscious and well, but was sitting up in bed and looked really well. I admit he was pale and looked exhausted, but to me he seemed fine.

"Thanks, Dennis," he said to me, "I understand you raised the alarm this morning?"

"Yes, but you would have done the same!" and we both smiled. "Anyway," I said, "we can move up in the world from pedal bikes."

"Why, what do you mean?" Fred asked, genuinely curious, but with more than a hint of suspicion in his voice.

"We might be able to use a car. There's a car club we can join."

Fred suddenly threw me a very serious look: "Don't you dare go to the dam without me Dennis Hubbard!" to which we both laughed, as much from relief that Fred was clearly going to be fine as from anything else.

The doctor joined us and at his request I returned with him to his surgery at the end of the ward.

"You're clear. So can we have a pint from you now?" he peered over the top of his glasses, smiling, and ushered in a very good looking nurse with long auburn hair and spidery long legs who promptly sat down next to me and began the process of extricating precious AB negative blood from my arm.

"This will go down to Bulawayo. Only two per cent of the population have this blood group, did you know?"

"Yes, I know," I replied, with a just a hint of pride, "I was told this in the army."

After half an hour I was given tea and biscuits. I sat in a soft seat enjoying seeing the nurse busily clomping around the surgery in her flat black shoes and crisp white skirt, and I could hear loud moaning and complaining from many of the patients in the ward. I recognised one or two as some of the more regular bar flies at the club, who were now most likely very upset at the fact the club was open for the evening and they were not there. This reminded me I had to be there myself to work, so I said goodbye to Fred and ran straight to the club where I slipped behind the bar immediately. At seven o'clock, time was called in the club and we started throwing our customers out. As usual some had to be carried bodily and dropped out the front door, virtually unconscious.

While Fred was in the hospital all that week I spent some time after work in the bar talking to my boss, who I knew by this time as David Kaye. On the rare occasions he was not drunk he was good company and it was through him that I met some people who would be hugely influential to me for the remainder of my time in Africa. It was one night during that particular week that I was introduced to the Chairman of the Broken Hill Railway Recreation Club, a huge but very smart and authoritative man by the name of Roy Welensky. He was already into a dignified middle-age when I met him and he spoke with great authority on the state of the country and how it needed to be changed and modernised. He was heavily involved in the trade union movement and stated he'd been trying for years to get Northern and Southern Rhodesia, both quite separate entities at the time, amalgamated into one country. He commanded a great physical presence and stated his origins were Jewish and Afrikaner, but he also spoke with great enthusiasm and affection for Britain, though I don't remember him saying he'd ever actually been there. Inevitably we had long discussions about politics and the direction in which the British Empire was heading, with Africa's part in it. He was inspiring company and seemed incredibly focussed in his intentions.

I also met an Afrikaner, Pieter van der Merwe, who insisted on being known simply as 'Van'. I wasn't to know just how much of an influence Van and his family would later have on me. He was a very pragmatic man, also into middle age, handsome and quietly spoken, with sun-bleached blonde hair and a lithe, athletic build. He looked well for his years. His home was only a short distance away and he invited me to visit on numerous occasions before I finally relented and arrived there one night after the club had closed.

Van's house was huge by British standards, and even though it was dark when I first saw it I could see it was far grander and more imposing than the bungalow Fred and I were living in. There was a veranda all around it and a shallow sloping corrugated iron roof which overhung and protected the veranda completely, with large windows and wide steps up to the front door. I was met at the door by a very pretty young girl with the most gorgeous brown eyes and long curly blonde hair with some rich shades of auburn, who immediately told me her name, Charlotte. She was sixteen, and at first seemed quite shy and reserved.

I said to her: *"Hoe gaan dit?"* meaning 'How are things?' but I didn't get much of a reaction. She took my hand quite unselfconsciously and led me through the house. She began talking to me and asked me questions about England and she then told me how much she wanted to travel there as soon as she could. I noticed on that first meeting that there was something unnaturally quiet about her, a definite sullenness which began to dissipate from the moment we met. I didn't get much chance to reply to Charlotte before Van appeared and shook my hand.

"Thank you for coming Dennis let me introduce you to my wife, Goldie," and I followed him into the kitchen, our shoes clomping quite loudly on the cool, polished wood floor. Mrs van der Merwe was a huge woman, not detracting from the fact that she appeared rather solid and healthy. She was as tall as she was wide, and looked strong enough to be able to pick me up with one hand if she wanted to. I decided right there and then that I would avoid picking a fight with this woman! I assumed 'Goldie' was a nick-name, as she had masses of thick strawberry blonde hair, which was clearly the reason for the name. I never knew her as anything else.

"I hope you have a good appetite tonight, Mr Englander!" she said, in a very clipped South African accent as she tended to some enormous steaks sizzling, spitting and smoking profusely on a huge hot-plate, filling the house with a wonderful cooked meat aroma. I was immediately very hungry, and we were soon sitting down to eat in their dining room. I met their son, Junior, who was Charlotte's older brother and had a keen interest in photography. He even had his own dark-room in the house where he developed all his pictures himself. He also played cricket and was anxious to find out if I played.

I don't think I'd ever eaten so much steak in one sitting before. My jaw ached from all the chewing, and yet more and more was dropped onto my plate. It tasted wonderful though, and it was a shame that Fred was missing out, lying in his bed at the mine hospital. I thoroughly enjoyed that first meal in Van's house with his family, and it was a taste of home life that I'd been missing since I'd arrived months before. After the meal two packs of cards were brought out and we played canasta. I hadn't played before but I'd seen some of the passengers on the *Capetown Castle* playing it, as it seemed to be incredibly popular at the time. Van partnered me in the first game against Goldie and Junior until I understood it, or at least thought I did. It was a very long, drawn-out game, and seemed to go on for hours. Charlotte sat with us, next to me, and helped her dad teach me the game.

I briefly mentioned to Van that Fred and I had been on cycling trips into the bush and Van seemed genuinely interested, and was far from critical, as others had been. He was even quite positive and encouraging. He was horrified however, to learn that neither of us had a firearm when on our little expeditions.

"Go to the mine, to the armoury. Give them my compliments, and make sure they sort you out with a decent rifle each, right?" and he was quite insistent, "There's no way you should go out there naked like that, without a gun…" and I nodded politely, not really knowing at that stage whether I would heed this advice or not.

I asked Van about his origins and how he and his family had ended up in Broken Hill, but he was very evasive and I never really managed a straight answer from him. Charlotte was more forthcoming and told me that both she and her brother attended a private school in Broken Hill, and would eventually find a place at a university somewhere in South Africa. Finally our card playing came to an end. It must have been close to midnight when both Charlotte and Junior asked if they could show me around the house, but the peremptory tone in Goldie's voice put an end to the evening with: "It's too late now, say goodnight to Dennis!" and with that they both disappeared up the stairs. I thanked Goldie and Van for a wonderful evening and made my way back to our bungalow. Curious thoughts filled my head about Van and his family, and about Charlotte. I'd never met anyone quite like them before. Our meeting seemed strangely prescient, as though we were fated to meet. I could feel this quite inexplicably strong at the time, but I wasn't to know then quite how true these feelings would become.

The next day was a great day. Fred came home from hospital.

MULUNGUSHI DAM

I booked a car for the following Saturday. What a wonderful feeling it was, ordering a car, reserving it for me and my friend. No questions were asked other than our names and where we worked. It must have been assumed that Fred and I could drive, as neither of us was ever asked to produce a driving licence of any sort. It was a good job we didn't, because at the time neither of us had one! I hadn't done any driving in the army, and so my only experience of driving anything was when I was fifteen and helped to manoeuvre the milk trucks around the dairy yards and farms near Sheffield. I was once tasked in driving a huge milk lorry six miles across Sheffield and did it all the way in first gear, unable and unwilling to risk the necessary double de-clutching in order to change gear. However, the car we were given the loan of was an imported 1946 Standard-Triumph *Flying Eight*, in a very drab earthy brown colour, and had synchro-mesh, so this wouldn't be a problem. It had been brought from England and was in remarkably good condition, with part-wood dashboard and leather upholstery. It was almost completely devoid of rust, but it did have a few minor dents here and there. To us though, at that time, it was a fantastic machine.

We both sat in the car trying to work out how to drive it. It was decided that I should drive initially, as my vast milk lorry experience when I was a teenager made me by far the more experienced driver. I familiarised myself with the foot pedals and the gear stick but couldn't work out the function of a large black handle which dropped from the roof between the two front seats. It moved around and obviously had some purpose. At first I thought it was the handbrake, but it didn't seem to be connected to anything, and besides, the car already had a handbrake. After ten minutes or more, Fred climbed out the car and looked at the roof. The mysterious black handle was connected to a moveable spotlight that neither of us had noticed, like a third headlight, mounted on the roof. We immediately and very ambitiously thought of how useful this could be at night, when hunting for wild game.

We still hadn't yet worked out how to start the car. We'd been given some keys to unlock the doors but I couldn't see where the ignition was. Then I realised there was a push-button the size of an old penny in the dashboard. This was the same as how the old milk truck used to start, so with my foot firmly pressed down on the accelerator pedal I shoved my right index finger onto the button and it fired into life on the first attempt. I'd forgotten to depress the clutch and so the car shot ten feet forward in one almighty lurch before I realised it was in gear. Luckily there were no obstacles or unsuspecting pedestrians in front of us and so I pretended this was my normal method of starting, and carried on driving, despite us both sustaining first degree whiplash.

The car had a huge engine by today's standards, a three and a half litre, so it was quite noisy and produced a fair amount of smoke. I fought with the controls as though in a wrestling ring and pointed the car both by accident and design in the general direction of our bungalow. I glanced briefly at Fred's face and saw that he looked absolutely terrified. He had one hand on the door handle and the other on his seat, and I could see the bones in his knuckles glistening white through his skin he was holding on so tightly. He'd gone very pale, almost ashen.

"Maybe we should go to the dam by bike?" he shouted, not taking his eyes away from where we were going, and looking as though he was about to open the door at any moment and leap out.

"It's alright, there's no problem. I've got the hang of it now," I replied, rather optimistically. I had, really, and it was only a few minutes later that we saw our bungalow appear on our right. Unfortunately my foot missed the brake pedal and we drove straight past, both of us turning our heads together and looking indignantly at our front door as it disappeared behind us.

I drove the car around Broken Hill on the pretext of gaining some extra driving practice, and made another approach to the bungalow, like a pilot trying to land a damaged aircraft. With the clutch down and footbrake depressed I steered the car successfully right up to our front door. We came to a steady stop and I turned off the engine. We sat for a moment in silence. Fred let out a withering sigh followed by more silence, and then:

"Right, let's load the car and get on with it, shall we?" and he looked at me with something of a forced smile and raised eyebrows. I could see he wasn't particularly happy, but I think his desire to get to the dam outweighed any further thoughts of my precarious driving.

Over the previous few weeks we'd managed to scrounge or otherwise purloin everything we needed for a successful trip. We had food, water, petrol, spare clothes, two second-hand fishing rods, reels, bait, spinners, and a map. We had to return the car before dark hence a very early start. There were still a couple of things we needed, and we left the collection of these until last. After successfully loading the car we drove over to the mine, in search of the armoury. Van had given me directions and I drove the car slowly past the gates into the mine complex and quite soon we came up to a single storey building that looked like a military style guardhouse, which we both guessed correctly could be the armoury. I stopped the car outside and I tossed a coin. I won. Fred went into the building. After ten minutes he'd still not come out. I was about to investigate when he emerged carrying two rifles in his arms, a small cardboard box, and a surprised grin across his face. He jumped in and I started the car. He didn't have to sign anything or pay a deposit, they apparently just handed them over to him, after mentioning Van's name. It was just after six o'clock in the morning, and we were off!

Fred stacked the rifles on the back seat and took out the map. On the southern edge of Broken Hill was a track which led south east towards Mulungushi Dam. Apparently if we followed this track for about thirty miles we would arrive at the southern end of the dam. Thirty miles doesn't sound far, and in Africa it certainly isn't. But the 'road' was no more than a dirt track and after the rainy season the surface was uneven and quite indistinct to say the least. There was just enough to follow as it meandered and weaved its way through the bush like some enormous flattened snake, disappearing briefly and then reappearing further ahead, just as we thought it had been lost. The only real positive in our drive through the bush was the fact that we were highly unlikely to meet any other traffic, so in this respect we could relax a little, as we had the track to ourselves. We'd been told that the faster we drove over the ruts and bumps the better, and then our momentum would somehow flatten out the surface. Sixty miles an hour was the speed we were recommended to drive at, but this just seemed impossible to achieve on such a road and in the *Flying Eight.* But we had to give it a go.

Once we were established on the track in first gear we gathered speed, up into second, then third, and finally fourth gear. We whipped past bushes and trees and we really did bounce over most of the ruts in the road. There were some uncomfortable noises coming from under the car but no matter how I pushed it we couldn't reach sixty miles an hour. The best we managed was fifty on a few occasions, and even that was an astonishing achievement. As we blundered through the bush at high speed I noticed Fred looked absolutely terrified. At one point I'm sure he even had his eyes tightly shut. There were occasions when I too was rigid with fear, but because I was behind the wheel I felt more in control, as you do when you are the driver in those circumstances. Such moments of terror can easily turn into extreme comedy, and we both occasionally laughed quite hysterically as we tore past yet more trees and bushes and tall grass by the road. God only knows what would have happened if we'd run into an elephant crossing our path.

I was amazed the car held together, but after half an hour of this white-knuckle rally driving we saw the surface of the dam ahead of us glistening in the morning sun. I slowed the car right down in order to find somewhere to pull up near the water's edge. Finally we arrived at a point that became familiar to us in subsequent visits and I stopped the car. We sat for a moment in silence with the engine off, completely in awe of the view. We climbed out and both stood overlooking the dam, staring at the scene in front of us. It was the most peaceful, the most beautiful stretch of water I'd ever seen in my life. There was absolute silence and no sign of anyone else around, either then, or at any time before our visit. It seemed this was a secret, undiscovered paradise that now belonged entirely to Fred and me, as though we were the first to ever discover it. Completely unprompted Fred took hold of my right hand with his and shook it warmly:

"Thanks Dennis, thanks for bringing me here to see this. It's just out of this world!" but I was speechless and just stood very still, staring at the water and the surrounding rocks and trees. I briefly thought of pit hill and pit pond back in Sheffield, and how much I'd loved those places. What I then saw before me was a thousand times better.

After weeks spent in a hot and stuffy office, this was the real Africa we had been looking for. We walked up to the water's edge and peered into it. I'd never seen water as clean in all my life and it just dropped down, deep, utterly gin clear. The sun was rapidly climbing high up above us in the deep blue sky and the day was becoming very warm. I felt a very strong urge to jump in, but we'd been warned about the local wildlife, hippos, baboons, and even crocodiles, though none were evident at that moment. My mind was racing with ideas. We had to get a boat of some kind and bring it to the dam, I had to bring a kite and fly it from the ridge above the water. We had to get the fishing gear out and make a start; the dam must have been full of fish!

We decided to explore the area first and find the highest point so we could see as much of the dam and lake as possible. We walked high above the water to a ridge from which we could see for miles in all directions. The lake stretched away far into the distance, and we knew it was about ten miles in total length, but we couldn't see all of it as it turned and twisted further away from the dam. The dam itself was not some distinct stone built wall but an even mound of grass-covered earth, clearly man-made but somehow also giving the appearance of a natural form, it blended so well with the landscape. It was all incredibly beautiful, and while we were utterly absorbed in our surroundings we were both startled back to reality by a sudden, very loud screech from the undergrowth just ahead of us. A huge, angry-looking baboon appeared from nowhere and started running straight toward us.

"Don't move!" Fred shouted, and at first I didn't know whether he was shouting this to me or the charging animal. Working on the principle that if we didn't antagonise it in any way it should hopefully leave us alone, we both stood still, rigid to the spot. This was the theory. I was frozen in my boots and my legs wouldn't move anyway, even if I'd wanted them to. The baboon ran incredibly fast right up to within a few feet of us and then turned sharply away at the last moment and disappeared again into the bushes. We were hundreds of yards from the car and neither of us had thought to bring a rifle. Clearly we had a lot to learn. I then remembered when I went for my short training course to Bulawayo I saw the train guard walking off down the track a hundred yards to change the points, and found it curious then that he was carrying a rifle. This was evidently more for reasons of protection against wild animals rather than a precaution against the train being robbed by human beings. As it became clear that the baboon had left us alone we both let out a sigh of relief and turned back towards the car, furtively and anxiously looking around us all the time. It could just as easily have been a lion, a cheetah, or a leopard that had just run out at us, but not, apparently, a tiger. Fred insisted there weren't any tigers in Africa. I argued the point, but he insisted.

At the car the first thing we did was take out the rifles. We loaded each one in silence, taking the box of cartridges from the car and slotting one into the breach. They were definitely not the same well-maintained Lee Enfield's we'd fired at the police station range. These were probably the same calibre but single-shot bolt-action guns, obviously quite old and very well used. Better to have these though than nothing at all, in the circumstances. I pushed the bolt forward and applied the safety catch, and Fred did the same with his. It was then that I felt some reassurance that Fred didn't drink; to be in the presence of a heavy drinker with a loaded gun in a pair of shaking hands was just unthinkable.

The encounter with the baboon made us think seriously about where we were. More because neither of us heard any sound of it until it screeched at us and was almost upon us. Clearly we had to be more alert and aware of our surroundings. We were not on some casual Sunday stroll in the park, this was the African bush, and we were in a wilderness were *we* were the trespassers into the animal's habitat.

We sat down by the water and drank Oros fruit juice, and ate some of the food we'd brought with us: bread, fruit, and 'biltong', which is strips of dried meat, and very tasty, once you'd become accustomed to it. We sat by the edge of the lake near a deep area of water, absolutely at peace with the world. I threw some biltong into the water as bait and then a spinner with some fearsome hooks attached, more out of curiosity than a serious attempt at fishing. It descended slowly until it was no longer visible. I'd never been fishing in such surroundings before, of utter peace and tranquillity. Fred and I talked about our time so far in Africa, and we both agreed that the dam was our greatest discovery. Sadly nothing was biting that day, and as the afternoon sun started to make its way westward we realised we'd have to return to Broken Hill.

Fred took a turn driving, and drove the car most of the way back without incident. We managed a more modest thirty miles an hour and successfully returned the car intact and undamaged at sunset. I handed the rifles in at the mine armoury to an indifferent response, and wasn't asked what we'd done with them or if we'd used them at all. I could see the armoury had a vast collection of weapons, enough for a small army. I knew there was a shooting club, but was still curious to know why they needed quite such an enormous arsenal of firearms at a mine.

We were both bursting to tell all about our trip to the dam, but decided to hold back and be quite selective in whom we informed, in order to avoid any undue criticism. Throughout the return journey we planned another trip to the dam, perhaps involving an overnight stay. In the bar that night Van came in and spent some time trying to make conversation with me while I was busy serving customers, and invited me to his house again for dinner. I was grateful for this as I had a tremendous appetite after the long days' adventures. At seven o'clock I left David, the bar manager, to evict the last of the customers and lock up the bar, and made my way across to Van's house. I felt relaxed in Van's home so I decided to discuss our trip to the dam. Van was very encouraging, though he did say:

"Dennis, you know you must always, I mean *always*, carry your rifle with you when you're out there, seriously!" as he shook his head very slightly, but then smiled, "I'm really glad you're exploring though, it's fantastic that you chaps want to do this. So many aren't even bothered about it you know." Goldie had been listening to our conversation, and was less encouraging, adding: "Yes, for sure, for an Englander like you, you seem to be really enjoying it, and I agree, it's great for you to see some of the country. But you need to be careful, I wouldn't go out there, it's dangerous you know."

Van then looked a little pensive but moved over to me and said: "We've got an old boat somewhere, a kayak, would you be interested in using it for your expeditions to the dam?"

I was absolutely thrilled and immediately retorted: "Yes, of course, that would be fantastic!" and I couldn't believe my luck.

"Right then, I'll drop it outside your bungalow tomorrow. But, just a little word of warning Dennis, when you're out on the water, keep a good look out for hippos, right?"

"Yes, alright," I replied, not really aware that hippos were dangerous. I thought crocodiles were the things to fear the most.

"You know they can be quite aggressive animals, and they're big heavy beasts," Van went on, sounding very sincere, as though speaking from some experience. I listened and made a mental note in order to pass the message on to Fred, as no doubt he was probably more worried about crocodiles, as I was.

"I'll get you some decent fishing gear too, we have some at the mine no-one seems to use."

"Thanks, Van," I said, excited about the prospect of telling Fred and then thinking ahead to our next expedition.

We finished our meal, steak again, and I declined a game of canasta. I was exhausted and so returned to the bungalow to give Fred the good news.

The Flying Eight.

THE POOL

Van called round to our bungalow with a beautiful kayak complete with paddles, and enough fishing equipment, much of it brand new, to last us a lifetime. Fred and I were desperate to return to the dam, but we had to wait several weeks for another car to become available. Our second adventure in the car was to be another all day visit to the dam. Meanwhile we still found new discoveries in and around Broken Hill. It was a Saturday afternoon when we first discovered the locally renowned Mrs English's Café. You know what it's like when you arrive in a new town and some of the buildings become familiar to you, even though you've no idea what they are. This was the case with Mrs English's Café. I initially thought the small detached shack of a building on the main street was a public lavatory; it certainly looked like one, until I saw the dirty and diminutive sign above the front window.

Mrs English was a big woman, as big as John Wayne's horse in fact, as I remember thinking at the time. But most horses were much better looking than she was. She had huge hair which balanced erroneously in a very suspicious manner on top of her head, the suspicions being vindicated when it seemed it was an entirely different colour, length, and style each day. But there were things living in the hair which attracted flies, as she constantly had clouds of them around her head, following her everywhere. Fred and I giggled furtively like a pair of schoolboys when we walked into her fine establishment and saw it for the first time, and the rest of Mrs English and her peculiar café. We sat down and noticed parts of the floor were literally an inch deep in dead flies, particularly near the front window. Mrs English seemed unconcerned as she came and went from the back room where the cooking was done, singing: "See what the boys in the back room will have..." completely off key and out of tune.

We tried some of her biltong, safe in the knowledge that she hadn't cooked it, and it actually tasted very nice, so we also bagged some up to eat later in the bungalow. The front door to the café was spring loaded so it slammed shut quite violently as soon as anyone came in or out, as though the flies inside were deliberately being held hostage in the building. Mrs English *always* had a long, thick, foul-smelling Turkish cigarette clenched between her thin lips, and her tanned face was creased and stained from an obviously excessive nicotine habit. I realised where I'd seen her before, and in fact she recognised me too, as she was sometimes a customer in the railway club. This became an occupational hazard, working behind a bar in the only drinking den in the town, where everyone then gets to speak to you at some point and they think they know you. She was pleasant enough, and I knew then that she liked a drink, scotch, usually, and plenty of it. There were so many huge flies in the café the air was thick with them, along with the perpetual sound of buzzing wings all around us. A very brave soul at the next table was eating a meal which appeared to consist of fly soup; steak and kidney fly pie, followed by blue-bottle current pudding. It was extremely hot in there too, and after twenty minutes we could stand it no more.

Daily life in Broken Hill became so good it was as though we were living in an unreal dream world, some kind of sun-drenched fantasy. Once April was over it just seemed to stop raining altogether, and any clouds were thin and wispy, drifting harmlessly overhead. I'd never known anything like it, as even on the rare occasions we had a dry summer in England it was usually punctuated by cloudy days with at least *some* rain. But this was not the case in Africa; here it just didn't rain at all, for months.

Fred and I worked in the same office building, in different offices, and every weekday we finished work at three-thirty. We then made our way to the huge open air swimming pool, a short walking distance away, to spend the rest of the afternoon jumping or diving from the high board, showing off, swimming, or lazing around in the sun. It was an idyllic lifestyle. The pool was shared between us railway workers, and those from the Broken Hill mine, all the white European workers that is. I never saw any black Africans in the pool, or anywhere near it. It never occurred to me, to be honest, why this was. I wonder now what would have happened if a black man had turned up in his trunks carrying a towel asking for a swim. I'll never know the answer to that, because it just didn't happen.

I clearly remember the first time I took off from the high board at the pool. There was only the one diving board, at the top of the steps at least fifteen feet above the water. I'd never jumped or dived from anything like it before. The view from the top looking down at the water was terrifying, and seemed a great deal higher from up there than from the ground. Standing at the top I decided to try a dive rather than a simple jump. I was conscious of an audience gathered around the board and bobbing about in the water. I nudged my toes over the edge of the board, feet together, and raised my arms out to my side. The end of the board wobbled but I didn't try to deliberately add any significant bounce to my dive. With my heart so far up into my mouth I could almost taste it and feel it beating in my throat, I pushed off from the end of the board and launched myself skywards. I have to say that as usual with a lot of my antics, I hadn't the slightest clue what I was doing. I leapt high into the air and attempted what I thought would become a beautifully graceful swallow dive, but gravity had decided to ruin this for me and I fell headlong into the water just managing to bring my arms around in front of me in time. It felt like I flew through the air for ten seconds or more, but it could only have been a moment, and I hit the water with incredible force and was sent deep down towards the bottom of the pool. I'd been told it was eighteen feet deep, and when I opened my eyes in the water I could see I was almost at the bottom. I panicked a little when I realised how deep I was, but allowed myself to float slowly towards the surface. There was a flutter of polite applause and some laughter from people around me.

I was thrilled and decided immediately to have another go. The pool was very popular and just as I was climbing the ladder back up to the high board someone challenged me to dive for a small 'Ticky' three penny South African coin. Of course I accepted the challenge and the Ticky was thrown into the water directly under the board. I briefly saw the small silver coin twinkle and flash in the refracted sunlight as it flipped and weaved its way to the bottom. I stood with my toes over the edge again, and looking down I was sure I could see it lying on the rough concrete floor of the pool. I decided I would maintain eye contact with it so I dived in, eyes wide open. Again I hit the water with tremendous force, but this time I felt as though my eyelids had been peeled back right over my head. I couldn't see anything at all for a few seconds and when I surfaced quite a few people at the poolside had clearly found my diving very funny as some were laughing hysterically. My sight slowly returned and I was informed my eyes were completely blood-shot.

A short while later – and when I'd fully regained my sight – I redeemed myself by recovering the Ticky from the bottom, after several others had tried and failed. It was tremendous fun, and my diving improved greatly through plenty of practice, in those long hot sunny afternoons spent by the pool, and all day at weekends.

THE KAYAK

The weekend finally arrived when we could collect and load up the car. I could hardly contain my excitement. I felt so cocky and self-confident that I even volunteered to collect the rifles and ammunition from the armoury. When I walked in and made the request, mentioning Van's name again, it was clearly a lot of trouble for them to step a few yards into the back room, and I was kept waiting at the desk for several minutes. The armoury was run by Afrikaners who seemed reluctant to speak to me in English. I hadn't yet picked up enough Afrikaans to speak back to them with any confidence, but this and our association with Van was soon turned to our advantage as the huge Afrikaner in charge said: "You've been here before for these haven't you?"

"Yes, a few weeks ago…" I replied, wondering where his question was leading.

"You're the friends of Mr Van de Merwe?"

"Yes, we are," I replied, nervously.

"I suppose you're going to want them again too, am I right?"

"Yes, if that's alright?" I replied, slightly more on the defensive.

"Right then," he said, leaning forward with the two rifles in his hands, "You hang on to them, keep them, but make sure you keep them safe in case we ask you for them back, alright?"

"Yes, fine, thanks," I replied, quite shocked, but nonetheless pleased.

I was handed a small but very heavy cardboard box and he looked at me and said: "If you need any more ammunition, come and see us again, right?"

I took the box of ammunition and with the rifles I made for the door. I didn't have to sign anything or give any written assurances. I loaded them into the car.

"Which one do you want?" I said to Fred.

"Either, I'm not bothered."

"No, I mean which do you want, *to keep?* We can *keep* the rifles, he's just told me."

"Really, are you sure?" Fred was as surprised as I was. "Well, as I said, I'm not bothered, you choose."

"We'll have to have a good look at them and test them out," I replied, starting the car. The nose of the kayak hung over the front of the windscreen slightly, tied to the roof of the car. I got out and secured it with some more rope. I then suggested Fred drive us to the dam in order to gain some more experience, and he edged over into the driver's seat.

We managed thirty miles an hour again on the rutted road and arrived at the dam in mid-morning. It was just as beautiful as ever, and the calm water was perfectly reflecting the clear blue sky above. Fred stopped the car at the bottom end of the dam in the same newly familiar place as before. We untied the ropes and lifted the kayak from the roof of the car and placed it on the ground.

"Been in one of these before?" Fred said to me.

"No. You?" I said

"No. Maybe we should have a go on dry land first, what do you think?"

"Yes, good idea," I said, stepping over to the rear of the kayak and climbing in. Fred stepped into the front, sitting on the pale green canvas-covered seat. As soon as we'd both sat down the kayak rolled over to one side. Not a good start, but a good job it was on dry land. We tried a second time. Again it rolled over as though in slow motion and tipped us both out onto the grass.

"Maybe it won't do it in the water?" Fred suggested. So we picked it up and carried it to the water's edge. There was no alternative to this, because if we accepted that it rolled over all the time it would mean we'd brought it for nothing and it was useless. But there was a risk if it capsized we'd be vulnerable to anything in the water that wanted to take a bite out of us. But we had to try, the curiosity was just too much to resist. A few yards along we found a shallow beach area where we could launch our little boat. We lowered it into the water and pushed it very gently a little deeper. It floated alright anyway, with no apparent leaks. Walking into the water up to his knees I held onto the kayak while Fred lifted a leg and climbed into the front. It took his weight with no problem. I let go, with fingers crossed, and amazingly it remained remarkably stable in the water. Fred and I looked approvingly at one another. Clearly it was alright after all. I climbed into the rear behind Fred. Again it took my weight with ease and it remained perfectly stable.

Above us on a ridge overlooking the water I suddenly saw that we had an audience. Half a dozen baboons were staring intently at us, looking very human as they were obviously keen to see what we were doing. I suspect there were very few, if any, visitors to the dam, and so we were clearly attracting a great deal of attention. They stayed on the ridge and were no threat to us at all, but as I acknowledged this fact I realised that yet again we'd wandered well away from the car, away from all our provisions, and our rifles.

We drifted quickly but smoothly quite far into deep water towards the middle of the lake. I looked around by my side where I was sitting and then said to Fred: "Pass me a paddle," assuming he had them at the front with him.

There was a moment's silence, and then: "I haven't got a paddle. I thought you had them,"

"I haven't got any, unless they're already in the kayak somewhere…" and I searched around on the floor of the kayak, but I knew with an awful realisation that they weren't there. We'd left them in the car. We'd therefore drifted close to the centre of a potentially dangerous lake in a kayak without a paddle between us.

"Shit," I said, and then: "Shit!" again. Nothing else seemed appropriate. "We need to get back to where we started," I murmured, almost to myself, and stating the obvious.

"Use your hands, Dennis," Fred replied, quite calm and phlegmatic as usual, and he had already started to do so, though worryingly he wasn't making the kayak move at all.

"Let's do it together, then we might get it going," I said, trying to stay calm. In unison we leaned over opposite sides of the kayak and carefully immersed our arms in the water right up to the elbows. Cupping our hands we heaved them through the clear water in long sweeping arcs while keeping a constant lookout around us. Eventually our timing was perfect and we finally began to make some progress. Plenty of people had warned us of the dangers of wild animals in and around the dam and up until that point we'd only seen baboons, but suddenly the warnings were in the forefront of my mind. Fred was very quiet as we paddled quite noisily towards the safety of the side. If there were any crocodiles or hippos in the lake then what better way to announce our presence than splashing about in the middle sticking our arms repeatedly into the water in an open invitation to lunch? At an agonisingly slow pace we dragged the kayak across the surface of the lake, clumsily but methodically, until finally it grew close enough to jump onto solid mud. We both climbed out quickly and pulled the kayak a little way up to stop it drifting away. In silence we both approached the car.

"What do we need?" Fred asked,

"Apart from paddles?" I laughed.

"Just the paddles and some water, maybe," Fred said. "We don't need the rifles, not on the water. Or do we? What do you think? Shall we take some fishing gear though?" Fred's voice was edged with more than a trace of relief and nervousness. I replied: "Yes, good idea, we could try some fishing out there on the lake. And yes, I think we should take at least one of the rifles. I'll carry the water on my back; you take a rifle on yours, right?" I could see Fred nodding in agreement, even though I wasn't sure what we could do with a rifle if we were attacked in the kayak. It was more for reassurance than anything else.

We loaded the kayak and set off again, using the paddles to shove ourselves firmly off the mud. We drifted, but in a more controlled fashion, back into the centre of the lake. We were both very quiet, and I think we were more than a little spellbound by the whole experience, in particular the silence, and the sheer tranquil beauty of the lake. We practiced using the paddles in long co-ordinated movements and surprisingly quickly it seemed as though we'd been rowing partners for years.

We raised our paddles into the kayak and sat completely motionless, soaking up the silence. 'Baboon Ridge' as we now called it passed behind us on our right, as we moved further down the lake, and our audience didn't follow but sat staring blankly at us. After what seemed hours but was probably only ten minutes or so, we paddled on. The lake just seemed to stretch for miles, and every few minutes one of us would suggest we turned back, but each time the other would reply:

"Just a little further…"

We'd been paddling for over half an hour, now with almost effortless expertise and co-ordination, when we came quite close to a wide muddy area on our left. The shore was about a hundred yards away at least, but suddenly the distance was nowhere near enough. Fred saw them first. I didn't give them a second look, as I missed them completely; I thought they were logs or branches from a tree. Three enormous crocodiles lay motionless in the mud at the water's edge; mouths open slightly, rows of teeth visible.

"Turn around, slowly. We've got to get back," Fred said, in a quiet voice, hardly more than a whisper. The crocodiles remained still, as we dipped the paddles into the water very carefully on one side, causing the kayak to turn very gently. We paddled quickly but quietly and the kayak drew away from the mud flats and the crocodiles. I had a sudden terrifying thought that if we then sank for some reason, we would have both been ripped apart and made an easy meal for our friends in the mud.

Luckily we were not pursued back up the lake, and we decided to go all the way back to the car, to our original launch area. I remember rowing back across the water in a tentative, slightly delicate manner at first, which soon began to speed up as we rowed on, further from the mud flats. I peered over the side of the kayak almost every time I dipped my paddle into the water, conscious of where I was putting it, and wondering whether anything would be there with lots of sharp teeth staring back up at me.

the Kayak.

THE RIFLES

We sat near the car eating lunch. Both of us were very slightly subdued but in quite a positive way. I think this was the actual moment when we finally realised we were in a potentially dangerous place. Fred told me about some new friends he'd made in his office at work, Alec and Diana. They were a married couple who Fred told me had become firm friends with him. He spoke with particular enthusiasm about Diana:

"They're good company, and she's very nice, but there's nothing in it you know," he said to me, completely out of the blue.

"There's nothing in what?" I said, a little confused.

"Well, Diana's very nice, but they're happily married of course…"

"Well, good for them," I said in reply, not particularly interested.

"Yeah," Fred went on, "anyone would have to be mad to start anything like that, with a married woman I mean," and I agreed. We'd both heard some stories of fights between husbands and even shootings when affairs came to light. The lifestyle we were leading, the booze, and the African heat clearly drove some people slightly mad. We made a pact between us, right there at Mulungushi Dam, that neither of us would ever get involved in anything of that sort.

I looked around and broke some branches from a nearby tree. I didn't tell Fred what I was doing, but I had a fantastic idea. He was sitting in the car, doors fully open, quietly inspecting the rifles.

"There are some gorgeous girls working in our office upstairs, Dennis. What about you, any in your office?" and I heard him pulling the bolt of the rifle backwards and forwards, and the clicking of the trigger in the empty breach.

"There's a few," I said, thinking, staring up at the blue sky.

I smiled and said: "There's one in particular, Sheila Ormiston I think her name is. But she wouldn't even let me in the front door, I know she wouldn't. Besides, I think she's attached anyway."

Fred stood up, and held a rifle to his shoulder: "We should keep at least one of these loaded at all times, Dennis, don't you agree?" he said, sounding very assertive and positive.

"Yes, right, but I've got an idea," I said, snapping some long branches across one knee and ripping the leaves off. I found an ideal branch about six feet long and trimmed the ends with a knife. One end was in a Y-shape and was just what I wanted. I took another straight branch and snapped off the end and tied a piece about a foot long across to form a T-shape at the end. A few minutes later I'd finished.

"We'll be alright, with these!" I proclaimed to Fred, and stood proudly in front of him with a stick in each hand.

"What on earth are they then?" Fred asked, genuinely baffled.

"This is the anti-snake stick," I said, demonstrating with the Y-shaped end a method of prodding at a snake, "You can get the snake by the head, like this, see?" as I made quick jabbing movements at the ground with my brilliant snake restraining device. "Then, if a croc comes at you, you can switch to this one," and I dropped the snake stick in favour of the other, and started making thrusting movements in front of me, "When the croc gets close enough, you ram the stick into its mouth and hey presto, it can't close its jaws, so then it can't bite me, you, or anyone else!"

Fred had watched me messing about with a couple of sticks while he sat with both our powerful rifles in his hands. He stared for a moment at me and my sticks, the water, and then at the rifles. I didn't realise what was happening to Fred at first but he began to cough and splutter uncontrollably as though he was falling into a seizure. He fell to the ground laughing so much his face streamed with tears. I was not in the least amused and thought my inventions were going to prove invaluable.

"Here," said Fred, trying to compose himself, passing me

one of the rifles, "If the damned thing is close enough as all that, then you'd shoot it, surely?" and he continued laughing. He picked up the other rifle and searched around in the tall grass near the car briefly then picked up a lump of wood the size of a football and launched it overarm in a great arc towards the lake. It landed squarely with a neat splash which sent perfectly round ripples all the way to the side closest to us in the calm water. Fred disappeared into the car and returned with the small cardboard box of ammunition.

"We need to make a start, so here goes," he said, and he took a bullet from the box and inserted it into the breach of the rifle and threw the bolt firmly forward. Standing fully upright he pulled the trigger and the gun went off with a deafening crack. The target in the water disappeared completely in a huge plume of spray as though hit by a small bomb. But the wood was untouched. The bang from the rifle came back at us immediately, echoing sharply from baboon ridge, and then again from further down the lake. The noise destroyed the silence around us and birds took to the air from the trees for hundreds of yards or more. Fred loaded and fired a second time, and again the spinning .303 bullet threw up masses of white spray when it hit the water.

"Come on, Dennis, give it a go," Fred said, "see if you can hit it!" I drew the rifle to my right shoulder and slotted a bullet into the breach. I aimed at the log and slowly squeezed the trigger. I was pleased to see the log explode with fragments and splinters flying off all across the water. It was great fun. I fired again and hit it again.

After half a dozen shots each I shouted to Fred: "Target destroyed!"

THE KITE

We sat down by the lake assessing one another's shooting skills, or lack of them, and Fred laughed again about my snake stick and croc stick inventions. He then said something very profound, and it was a statement that I remember to this day as though he'd only just said it:

"You know, this is all so perfect, I'd rather die right here, and be a victim of our friends back there on the mud flats than die a sad and lonely old man." It wasn't until much later in life that I fully understood this statement.

The sun was high above us, a bright yellow sphere in the centre of a gorgeous deep blue sky. There was a slight breeze now and I could see the tops of the trees up on baboon ridge in the near distance jiggling around and bending slightly, and then I remembered I'd brought the first kite I'd made in Africa.

"Let's go up onto the ridge and fly the kite," I suggested, as I stood up and was already moving toward the car. It may seem odd looking back now, to modern 21st century eyes, two grown men wanting to fly a kite. Maybe it was odd, but this was a simpler time before computers and mobile phones, when pleasures were simpler, and entertainment had to be homemade, just like my kites.

"Right," Fred replied, "but I'm taking this with me!" as he took hold of the green webbing sling of his rifle and threw it onto his back. He then took a handful of bullets from the box and dropped them into his shorts, where they rattled and jostled around for the rest of the day in his deep pockets with a tiny but reassuringly clangourous noise. I leaned into the car and took hold of my kite, a beautiful construction that old Joe Bar would have been proud of. It wasn't too big, about three feet across, made of the usual split bamboo cane and brown paper. I picked up the string and a few bits of cloth for a tail, and also the water bag. We both also stuffed strips of biltong under our belts in case we were hungry.

As we climbed up towards the ridge, our friends the baboons appeared ahead of us. They seemed very excited and jumped around screeching and running about like lunatics. But they kept their distance and seemed quite wary of us. We followed the same path up to the top of the ridge that we'd taken on our first visit and when we arrived there we realised just how breezy it was. Excellent conditions for kite flying! I tied the string onto the belly band of the kite and handed the kite to Fred, who walked off some way across the ridge. I unwound about a hundred yards of string and waited for a suitable gust.

"Now!" I shouted to Fred, as he stood with the kite at arm's length. Then I noticed he was holding it upside down, so I indicated for him to flip it over. Then he launched it up above his head and released it. The kite took off, high into the clear air, but started spinning uncontrollably, so I released the string and allowed it to touch down gently. I walked over to it and tied some cloth to a six foot length of string from the tail. It needed some weight. After a second launch it flew straight up and was firm and steady, catching the warm breeze perfectly. Fred looked suitably impressed. He came over and stood with me for a while and I showed him the rudiments of kite control: diving, turning, falling, climbing and so on.

We drew an audience on the ridge and the baboons sat staring at us. I don't think they'd even seen the kite at this point so I decided to have some fun with them. Using the wind direction and the fact the baboons were right on the top of the ridge, I managed to pull the kite down very low over their heads from behind them. The tail cloth hanging from the kite flapped onto the back of one of the unsuspecting baboons who immediately struck the animal next to him probably in the mistaken belief it has he who had just hit him. I kept the kite low over their heads and the bit of cloth danced around amongst the baboons as they tried to jump up at it, pushing one another in the process. Very soon they were screeching wildly, hitting one another and going absolutely berserk, making a tremendous noise and commotion. It was a hilarious sight, and a real shame Fred hadn't brought his camera. Eventually the whole group broke out into a jumbled, rolling fistfight, and the tumbling mass of hairy arms and legs ran off screaming into the bush. I hauled the kite skywards again and it climbed quickly on the breeze.

It was then that I first noticed several small brown human faces peering at us through the bushes only fifty yards away. I had no idea where they'd come from, but I whispered to Fred that we were being watched. They seemed completely bemused by the kite, which by now was probably fifty or sixty feet in the air above us. Fred acknowledged that he could see our new audience, so I decided to have some fun with them too. I tied the string securely to a bush and we both walked away. The kite was hanging beautifully in the air, perfectly balanced, so I was confident it would stay up there. Fred and I walked about thirty yards and then hid in the undergrowth with a reasonably clear view of the end of the string.

As soon as we were apparently out of sight a small group of perhaps half a dozen young native African boys emerged and walked cautiously towards the string. They gathered around it, occasionally staring up at the kite. They were of varying ages, from five or six up to eight or nine, and the only clothing they had on was some very tatty shorts, and nothing at all on their feet. They were giggling and constantly looked around them and then up at the sky. One of them reached forward and with an outstretched finger pulled quickly at the string. The kite dived momentarily but then resumed its position in the clear blue sky, as though nailed into place. The boys jumped around in absolute fits of laughter. The same boy then grabbed at the string again, holding onto it a little longer before releasing his grip, watching the kite dive and then resume its position. He'd probably never seen a kite before but had already worked out the basic principles. The younger ones again fell about in hysterics. Fred and I smiled and had to fight back some laughter, but we didn't want to do anything which may have frightened them away. We wanted to see where this would lead. Eventually they all had a quick pull at the string, and indeed they soon started pushing and pulling at one another in order to have repeated grabs at it. The older ones among them then held the string for several seconds, pulling the kite lower, and then releasing it, watching the cause and effect in their hands. We observed their antics for quite some time before we sadly realised we should start to make our way back to Broken Hill. I didn't want to disturb the boys so we sneaked away, leaving them with the kite.

*Top: My Broken Hill Railway Recreation Club Membership
Card. Bottom: Broken Hill pool*

With and without rifle, outside our bungalow 1951, my bike in the background against the wall.

Top: Standing in my garden outside our bungalow. Bottom:
Fred posing in the bush

Top: Self with Taffy and Bill near the pool,
Bottom: Taffy holding me up, by the pool 1952

Broken Hill Cricket Team c. 1952

Standing L. to R.   J.Hamilton,   W.H. Sheppard,   D. Hubbard,   R.J.S. Baker,   E.N. De Klerk,   D.W. Molver,   A. Metcalfe.

Sitting L. to R.   R.J. Andrews,   E.L.S. Baker (Capt.),   ? S Baker,   H. De. V. Moll(Vice Capt.)   M.V.S. Meyer,   W. Turner

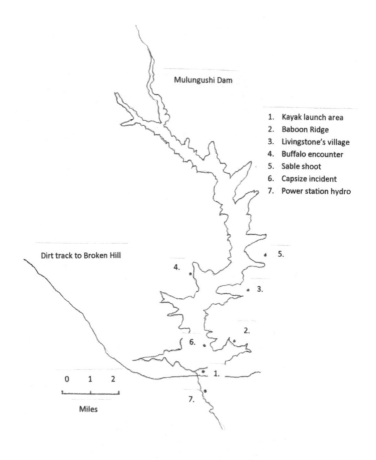

Mulungushi Dam

The envelope in which I sent the nylons from Elizabethville home to England

The photograph of Esther I took with me to Africa

Top: In my garden.
Bottom: The boat home: The Stirling Castle
Cape Town, Nov. 1952

The carved animals given to me by Livingstone in his village.

At Roy Welensky's grave, Dorset, England, 2006.

SONNY'S TRIP

It often seemed to me that having to go to work every day was a real intrusion into the perfect life in our African paradise. But the working days usually passed very quickly, and we almost always finished in mid-afternoon. I was constantly busy, which helped pass the time in the office, and there were always problems to resolve. The 'sheet-slashing' of the covered goods wagons was getting worse and consequently quite a lot of cargo was being stolen. Luckily the huge copper slabs were too heavy to be removed from the trains, so this at least was left untouched. I produced some quite shocking graphs of just how much was being stolen through 'sheet-slashing' and made a formal suggestion in writing for the railway to use closed vans in the manner of British Rail. If we couldn't use completely closed wagons then some boarding over the sides and top would certainly help. I received an acknowledgement of my suggestion, but as far as I know it was not acted upon. I discussed this with my boss, Sonny Amyot, and he was intrigued and I could see he was also impressed. I told him about our adventures at Mulungushi Dam, and the following Sunday he invited Fred and I to his house, promising to take us on a sight-seeing tour of his own.

We arrived at nine-thirty as requested. His house was similar in size to Van's but this was quite different in that it was built on stilts. The internal décor was minimal, almost sparse, and not as homely as Van's house. Sonny introduced us to his pretty wife, Sara, who seemed rather delicate and frail. I was later informed she was very ill, but I never found out why. We sat in the lounge room and their servant boy brought us coffee and some huge scones, made by Sara the day before. Sara spoke with a strong and mellifluous French accent and frequently conversed with her husband in French while we were there. If she knew what Sonny had planned for us I gained the distinct impression she didn't agree with it. After coffee and the wonderful scones we said goodbye to Sara and climbed into Sonny's car. The three of us chatted amiably on the journey, and I noticed we seemed to be heading east in the direction of Mulungushi Dam. Sonny refused to be specific as to what he had in store for us, but I could sense that he was excited and was clearly looking forward to it. After half an hour we turned away from the dam, more in a south easterly direction for another twenty minutes or so. The track eventually emerged into a wide clearing and Sonny stopped the car.

"Here we are, gentlemen!" he shouted, opening his door, "We're here."

I looked around and wondered where we were. There was nothing to see. Sonny disappeared to the back of the car and pulled out what appeared to be a wicker picnic basket. He spread a large blanket on the dry earth next to the car and took out a huge colourful map from the basket. He handed me a piece of fruit, plump and with a smooth, mainly yellow skin I'd seen before but not yet tasted, and then a knife, which I presumed was to cut the fruit with.

"This is my map," he said, proudly, opening it up carefully on the blanket, "When I first came here to South Africa thirty years ago, like you I found it fascinating. There were no detailed maps in those days so I decided to make my own, and here it is!"

Fred and I stared in awe at Sonny's hand-drawn map of the area, intricate, highly detailed, and very colourful.

"What are these red areas?" Fred inquired, seeing quite a few dotted across the map.

"Tsetse fly areas, to be avoided if at all possible," Sonny replied. "You can go there, but you have to be sprayed, otherwise you'll be ill."

I saw lines and arrows across the map with images of elephants, lions, giraffe and other animals. Sonny saw me looking and commented:

"These are the migration routes, Dennis. I soon realised the animals have specific places and movements throughout the wet and dry seasons, and the areas where they like to congregate. They are creatures of habit you know. For example, there are always lions in a place not far from here, I'd be happy to show you one day," and he leaned forward and pointed to a part of his map which looked suspiciously close to the dam and not far from our favourite place at baboon ridge.

Sonny cut a piece of fruit open and ate it, indicating for me to do the same with mine. I'd never tasted anything so marvellous in all my life. Sweet and juicy, better than anything I'd ever eaten before. I assumed it was a mango, but Sonny said: "You like your paw-paw, Dennis?"

"Yes, it's marvellous, thank you," I said, opening up the fruit to find two rows of large, black, bean-like seeds inside. I took one and surreptitiously slipped it into the pocket of my shorts, as though stealing it, with an idea to plant it somewhere later. Sonny handed a paw-paw to Fred who on opening it up and tasting it was equally enthralled. I ate another, and so did Fred.

"Where's your rifle?" I asked Sonny; sure that he must have one with him somewhere.

"I don't have one. Never have," he replied, with some pride in his voice. "I work on the principle that if you leave them alone, they should leave you alone. I know it's not the usual thinking back there in Broken Hill, but it works for me!"

I was impressed, and it certainly was an alternative way of thinking. Suddenly Sonny stood up:

"Right, come with me gentlemen, it's getting hot and I want to show you something, something that will cool you down a little." He folded his wonderful map and put it back in the car, then led us off into the bush. Fred and I followed in single file, entirely trusting in Sonny's leadership. As we walked Sonny told us a few interesting facts about the dam. He stated it had been built in the 1920's when GEC (the British General Electric Company) fitted a turbine room at the bottom of the dam to provide power to the Broken Hill mine.

"The turbines are fed by fast flowing channels of deep water from the dam," Sonny went on, as we followed him through the bush. I began to lose my bearings as we twisted and turned and pushed our way through some quite dense undergrowth. I wondered how far we were going until after a while Sonny stopped quite abruptly and looked down. He then said: "Here's one of them!"

The three of us were standing side by side overlooking a concrete channel about six feet wide, which was set at a shallow incline and was filled with fast flowing water. It appeared to be at least five or six feet deep and I noticed quite a few objects, both living and dead, were being swept along in the strong current at an incredible speed. Before we could see what he was about to do, Sonny was standing on the side wall overlooking the channel, bolt upright and completely naked. He dived headlong into the current shouting: "Follow me!" and he hit the water with a very awkward splash and was gone. Fred looked at me, and we realised that we had no choice but to follow. How would we get back if we lost Sonny? We both quickly stripped off and I noticed we each looked as though we were wearing white underpants due to our very prominent tan lines. We stood together on the side of the channel for a moment.

"We must be mad!" I shouted, before I stepped off, feet first, shouting: "Geronimo!"

As soon as I hit the water I was carried along in the current, and rolled over and over like clothing in a washing machine. I held out my arms to protect my head and dared not open my eyes. I could feel things, inanimate objects or living creatures, or both, passing me in the water, touching my skin as they did so. I shut my eyes and hoped for the best, there was nothing else I could do. I didn't know which way was up or down, and quite soon I felt the irresistible urge to take a breath. I bumped the side wall a few times and my arms protecting my head made repeated contact with the bottom of the channel. I had no idea where Sonny was or even if Fred had followed, I was so busy concentrating on trying to stay alive. For a few moments I thought my time had come. I had to take a breath soon or I was sure I'd drown, so I slowly opened my eyes. I was still being rolled over and spun around in the current, but managed to discern the surface simply because I could see the brightness of the sun above. I forced my arms to push my head towards the light, and with huge relief my head and shoulders suddenly broke the surface. I took a grateful gulp of air and quickly looked around me. I realised I was bobbing along in the current travelling at about fifteen or twenty miles an hour down the concrete channel. Overhanging trees and branches passed above on both sides and I remember thinking: *This is amazing!* Even though I had no idea where it was leading, how far, and what would happen at the end.

I sat in the current, treading water for what seemed several minutes, gliding along in the channel, until suddenly I noticed Sonny ahead of me, smiling, looking as though he was in front of a solid concrete wall.

"Get ready to stop, Dennis!" he shouted, "put your legs out in front of you!" and I did as I was told, just in time as I came to a sudden halt against a wall of steel bars. Bits of trees and detritus of all sorts were also gathered together and pushed against the bars with us.

"That was great, eh?" Sonny said, smiling broadly at me.

"Oh yes, fantastic!" I replied, clinging onto the bars. I could feel the full force of the water as it pushed against me and rushed around my body, through the bars and then down into the darkness of a huge enclosed pipe with a great roaring and rushing sound. It was rather a good job that the bars were there. Fred appeared, his head bobbing along towards us like a football, looking vacant and thoroughly traumatised, and we each shouted the same instructions at him. He thudded to a sudden stop against the bars next to us, and to my great surprise he started laughing a real hearty guffaw. He rubbed his face with one hand and looked at me.

"Dennis Hubbard, what the hell do you keep getting me involved in?" and with that, the three of us all started laughing as we clung together onto the cool steel bars.

Getting out involved a quick and easy climb up the bars and onto the wall of the channel. Then we had a long walk back through the bush to find and recover our clothes. There was no self-consciousness of being naked together, and we each talked loudly and with some relief about the channel. The common bond of a shared near death experience by drowning had obviously united us completely! Our clothes were exactly where we'd left them and we dressed while still talking animatedly about the channel, occasionally looking down at the water.

Back at the car Sonny opened the wicker basket again and revealed sandwiches, cooked chicken legs, cakes, fresh water, more fruit, and even wine. We sat near the car under the shade of a huge tree, and thoroughly enjoyed our lunch. After what we'd just been through, I think Fred and I were just glad to be alive!

After lunch we were on the move again. Sonny led us down a track on an incline which became quite steep in parts, to the extent that our ears popped a couple of times. Twenty minutes later we found ourselves stepping into a wide clearing where a peculiar red brick building emerged, looking completely incongruous in the African bush. With no windows visible, there were huge double wooden doors with polished brass handles which Sonny immediately opened. There was a plaque on the wall outside which simply read: 'G.E.C.'

We followed him inside and a white man in crisp blue overalls greeted Sonny enthusiastically and with great deference, as though they knew each other very well. We followed Sonny as he and the man in the overalls walked ahead of us, chatting to one another in Afrikaans. We descended some steps and through more double doors. I heard the sound of machinery becoming louder and then I saw some huge turbine generators in a cavernous turbine room.

"Here it is gents, the source of all my power!" and Sonny smiled, an arm raised up at the huge machines whirring away. "This is where all the electricity is generated for Broken Hill," he said, proudly, "Isn't it amazing?" he smiled, looking at us briefly, like the proud parent of a child prodigy, before becoming engrossed in conversation again with the man in blue. I was very impressed. I don't think I'd given it any thought, and had no idea where the electricity came from before then. We were allowed to wander around the turbine room for a while before being offered a coffee in a rather smart lounge room area. We sank into some deep and luxurious dark brown leather armchairs, and chatted to the man in blue about the power station. He asked us in a clipped Afrikaans accent how we liked life at Broken Hill, and I mentioned to Sonny that I'd met Roy Welensky, to which he threw me a withering look.

"Beware of that man," he said, suddenly serious, "he has some dangerous ideas," and he stood up, clearly a little agitated. I felt guilty I'd spoken about it and changed the subject immediately, but was surprised and suspicious as to why he clearly had little regard for Mr Welensky. I didn't feel as though I should pursue the matter, and so I left it.

The walk back up to the car was tiring, as of course it was entirely uphill, and very warm in the late afternoon sun. The drive back to Broken Hill was uneventful, and Sonny dropped us off at our bungalow at about five o'clock, just as the sun was setting. We thanked him profusely, and asked him to pass our thanks to his wife for the wonderful food.

"I've enjoyed your company," Sonny said to us both, "we don't mix with many Englanders usually, and it's been a good day."

I had to disappear to the bar almost straight away. Fred said he was going to turn in for the night, as he was so tired. When I returned just after seven o'clock Fred was out. I found a note on the table: 'Gone to Alec and Diana's for canasta – don't wait up!'

THE CONGO

Football and cricket were popular pastimes and I played in the Broken Hill Railway team for both. The nearby mine also had their own teams, and we frequently played some quite serious but friendly games, which usually finished quite evenly matched. In my first year I was lucky enough to be part of the football team tour when we were sent 200 miles north to Elizabethville just over the border in the Congo. Elizabethville was quite a large town at the time, probably bigger than Broken Hill, and was the capital of the southern Congo province of Katanga. This region was a pivotal area of the Copper Belt and so mining was a huge part of the local economy.

The train north was a huge old steam train: black, filthy, and extremely smelly inside, even more so than the one we'd travelled in from the Cape. The soot fell like rain as it heaved its way out of Broken Hill station with a cacophony of clunking, grinding and hissing like the formidable grand old lady she was. Luckily we only had to sit in the carriage for a single day's journey, and though it was still officially winter it was in the low seventies Fahrenheit and pretty airless inside. We chugged past Chibwe and Kapiri Moshi, small towns whose names had become familiar to me in the office, before we stopped at Ndola near the border for a crew change. I saw some black men in smart Congo Railway uniforms walking past towards the engine but I didn't appreciate the significance of this until later when we reached Elizabethville. Over the border into the Congo we passed through Sakania and then Tshinsenda, two more vaguely familiar names, until we reached our destination in mid-afternoon. It may have been my imagination, and even though we were only 200 miles closer to the equator, it seemed distinctly hotter and more humid than Broken Hill. But this was not the most important and notable difference from life in Northern Rhodesia.

After almost a year in Rhodesia and South Africa, where the indigenous black Africans clearly played a secondary role in everything and were not permitted to mix with the white population or hold positions of any status, we'd arrived in a country where the black people seemed to be far more noticeable. This discovery came as a complete revelation to me, as the segregated society was up until then all I'd known in Africa. Clearly this was not the case everywhere. The train driver had indeed been black, as were most of the staff at Elizabethville station. After we'd boarded a bus to take us to our hotel I saw the streets of the town populated by smartly dressed and confident-looking black people, and saw they were working in the shops and even driving cars around. This was something I had not seen before. Yet again I began to ponder some serious questions about the paradise I was living in over the border.

We were met by some very affable and smartly dressed white officials from the Congo Football Association, who seemed thrilled at our visit. The sun was setting quickly in the rapid African twilight and we were shown to our rooms by eager and extremely friendly black hotel staff. Our hotel was superb. We each had en-suite rooms with showers and they were clean and quite luxurious. Though I knew my teammates, Fred was not amongst them, so after a fabulous meal of steak and a fruit pudding, I decided to get some sleep.

I slept very well in a huge double bed and woke up bleary eyed and very hungry the next morning. Breakfast was fantastic and consisted of eggs, bacon, tea and toast, and plenty of it. We then had a team briefing in the hotel reception area. Our manager, an energetic Geordie called Jimmy Dodds, briefly explained the itinerary, and we then climbed aboard a bus bound for our first match in Elizabethville's main stadium. I was impressed by the football stadium, and it was probably big enough to seat 10 – 15,000 people. We changed quickly and ran out onto the pitch, eager to face our opposition.

The spectators were almost entirely black Africans. We visitors won the toss and did well in the first half, managing to get four goals past our opponents. The fair-minded crowd cheered and clapped every time we scored a goal, but at half-time we decided to perhaps allow the other team some generosity. Some of us actually voiced concerns about what might happen to us if we scored another four goals. Astonishingly the general consensus among our team was that we had to let some goals in or our personal safety might be at risk. There was no evidence of any sort to support this irrational fear, other than perhaps some simple prejudice and ignorance.

So we ran onto the pitch for the second half to an ecstatic crowd, determined to allow our opponents some face-saving, but without seeming to capitulate completely. Using a very blatant foul in our goal mouth a penalty was awarded to our opponents. The goalkeeper must have been distracted because even though the striker from the opposing team miskicked the ball terribly, causing it to roll very slowly towards the net at little more than a slow dribble, our goalkeeper dived headlong in completely the wrong direction. If he was being paid we would have sacked him on the spot. The ball rolled over the line so slowly it didn't even have the legs to reach the back of the net. The crowd suddenly went completely berserk. It was as though England had beaten Germany in a World Cup final, only much more animated. I was surprised the wooden stands could tolerate the amount of jumping about and heavy footfall on them without collapsing in a frenzied mass of timber and twisted limbs.

Our team kept possession for a while despite some very clumsy passing, and the ball somehow found the back of our opponent's net yet again. As the game restarted the host team gained in confidence, no doubt inspired by their amazing first goal, and coincidentally just as our keeper was unavoidably distracted by having to tie one of his boot laces their star striker and penalty taker took a shot which hit the cross bar before dropping into the back of the net. The already jubilant crowd went wild again, and soon after that the final whistle was blown and the game ended 5 – 2.

The next two days were very similar, but we played in small towns at exhibition matches around Elizabethville. Despite seeing local black people holding some responsible jobs we never saw any black football players. No doubt they did exist, but the mixing of the races on a recreational level clearly did not happen. We played a team of burly white miners in a nearby town called Kipushi, and lost 2 – 1. Many were Belgian nationals, and they were good players. Our reception at these games was always warm and friendly and each night we returned to our lovely hotel.

On the morning of our last full day, Jimmy Dodds came to see us just as we were finishing breakfast. He announced that we had one more match to play, but it would not be an easy game. Our hosts had apparently gathered together a team consisting of the best players from all the teams that we'd played so far. It would definitely be a tough match, but it was to be the ultimate decider between the home players and the visitors. This certainly roused our curiosity and we were all very excited about the game.

Until then we had a few hours' free time, so some of us walked into the town for a look around. Many of the shop workers were black and very helpful, and there was no shortage of things to buy. There were a huge amount of consumables imported from Europe and America, and I bought two pairs of American nylon stockings, one pair for my mother and the other pair for Esther. I posted them to Sheffield from Broken Hill the next day, at a cost in postage of two shillings and eleven pence.

I remember our final game very well, even to this day. We played in Newcastle United colours of black and white stripes, probably thanks to Jimmy's influence. The opposition played in a bright orange strip, and I've no idea if there was any significance to this colour. It was incredibly exciting and was probably the best football match I've ever played in. We won the toss and kicked off at two-thirty. It immediately started well for us and in particular for me, as even though I wasn't a striker I found myself in possession of the ball running alone straight towards our opponent's goal. I think I panicked a bit and took a shot a little too early. The light, dry ball took off clear over the keeper's head but sadly struck the cross bar and fell straight into the keeper's hands. I was fired up by this brilliant start though, and felt completely engaged in the match from then on. The crowd was very sporting, but quite often on occasions when one of the home team merely touched the ball they would cheer and clap wildly. Immediately after my shot at the goal I found myself being closely marked by a small Belgian man who followed me around as though attached to me on a piece of elastic. I couldn't get rid of him, as whichever direction I turned he was there, doing what he was supposed to be doing, getting in the way of me and the ball.

Our teams were pretty evenly matched and there had been few shots at the goal until just before half time when their right winger sent a beautiful cross from near the right corner post straight towards our goal. In the jostling scrum of players at the goalmouth our keeper completely misjudged the pace and direction of the ball and it hit him squarely on the back of the head, from where it went spinning straight into the net. The home crowd went wild, and then again a few minutes later with the blowing of the half time whistle at 1–0.

In the dressing room our manager, Jimmy, gave us a thorough pep talk in the manner of all football managers across the world when their team is losing at half time. There were some very colourful swear words involving sex, with threats and promises attached which involved knocking us down then building us up to such an extent that when we went back out onto the pitch we believed we could conquer the world. 'Positive motivation technique' I think it's called. It was decided that we'd not been nearly aggressive enough and from then on we were told: 'Take no prisoners'. I was all fired up and went straight for my little Belgian friend and almost broke his leg with a very nasty tackle which the referee can't have seen properly as it left him rolling around on the dusty dry grass in agony. This was how we played for a full thirty minutes after half time and it was eventually rewarded when one of our strikers, a particularly tall chap called Ken, caught a glorious pass from the centre and headed the ball into the middle of their net for the equaliser. There was polite applause and some cheering – or was it jeering – from the crowd before we kicked off again.

We tried to maintain the pace but after twenty minutes or so I began to tire, as did many of my fellow teammates. I slowed to a walk in order to catch my breath for a few moments, aware of a sudden raging thirst. Our captain, Les Vickers, a usually cool and phlegmatic man, ran up to me, with a beet red face and as lathered in sweat as a Derby Day race-horse:

"Are you alright, Dennis?" he enquired, appearing breathless and anxious as though he was just about to have a stroke, "It's just that you look a bit red," and he put an arm on my shoulder in a tentative but no doubt sincere gesture of reassurance. Clearly I must have looked as bad as him.

"I'm fine, thanks Les. You look a bit red yourself you know," and we picked up our pace and ran back towards the game.

"It's not long to go now, let's see if we can get another one past them!" Les shouted, with some very brave, fake sincerity in his voice. I didn't know whether our opponents were just fitter than us or were simply better players, or both, but quite soon it seemed there were orange shirts everywhere, as though they were playing with twenty men. They kept possession of the ball, passing it between them all the time in a very selfish and unsporting manner. Their side was slick and disciplined and all their players worked brilliantly together as though they'd been best friends for years. My Belgian friend was all over me again, and despite numerous attempts to trip him, much to the annoyance of the crowd, he didn't allow me to get near the ball again. In the last twenty minutes of the game the excitement was entirely in our half of the pitch, the ball being kicked around at or near our goalmouth until almost inevitably it was belted firmly and decisively into our net for a second time. A few minutes later the final whistle blew and the home side had won 2 – 1. The cocky visitors from over the border had been ignominiously thrashed. The crowd almost rioted with pleasure.

After a shower in the fantastic changing rooms we imagined we would be taken by bus back to our hotel or worse still, bundled onto the train straight away. But quite the opposite happened. We were taken to the best hotel in Elizabethville and treated to a formal civic reception. We ate a fabulous five-course meal in a huge resplendent room with chandeliers hanging heavily and majestically from a very high ceiling and a small orchestra playing in one corner. Quite by chance I sat next to my little Belgian friend, who at first I thought would be quite antagonistic or even downright rude to me, but he introduced himself as Maurice and told me in near perfect English just how much he'd enjoyed the game. He told me he was from Liege and was only halfway through a three year contract with a Katanga copper mine. He spoke wistfully of his home in Belgium and of his wife and two children he'd left behind. He was clearly missing them terribly and was very homesick. He also spoke about the Second World War and of living under Nazi occupation. I tried to steer him away from such topics and mentioned that Arsenal had won the FA Cup that year, which he already seemed to be aware of. He loved football and it was clear that playing the game and enthusing about it kept his sanity intact. I was encountering more Europeans who were struggling to cope with the heat and isolation of life in Africa, despite the almost indescribable beauty of the place.

We left the Congo the next morning. We'd had a truly wonderful time. I think I slept most of the day on the train, as did many of my teammates. On my arrival back at Broken Hill I posted the nylons to my mother, all those thousands of miles away in cold, grey England. Fred was keen to hear about my trip north, and listened intently. In return he told me excitedly of his long games of canasta with Alec and Diana and their friends.

MY GARDEN

My first winter in Africa, also known as the 'dry season', passed with a slight variation in the seasons but was like nothing I'd been used to. For a couple of the midwinter months, namely June and July, I suppose it did get quite cool at night, but by European standards it was never cold. It certainly never fell below fifty degrees Fahrenheit, or around ten degrees Centigrade, and it was still warm and dry during the day, in the seventies Fahrenheit, or high teens in Centigrade. But this was quite chilly after the usual temperatures of almost twice that number. In fact these winter months did remind me of a very good English summer, apart from the absence of rain! It was obvious from very early on that the climate was a grower's paradise, and that there would never be any of the gardener's worst enemy, by that I mean the dreaded night-time frosts. The well-trimmed privet hedges around our bungalows were not, on closer inspection, privet at all, but pomegranate bushes. Most of them had fruit on them too, which just seemed to go to waste. There were avocado trees and what I later recognised as paw-paw trees laden with fruit, and not apparently owned by anyone, just growing wild. I hadn't eaten an avocado before and this came as a real treat too, similar to my first paw-paw when on Sonny's trip.

During one of my early visits to Van's house I mentioned how favourable the climate would be to gardening and growing vegetables, and that I'd like to cultivate my own little garden. At first all present simply laughed and questioned why anyone would want to take the time and trouble to grow anything for oneself, when food was plentiful. Besides, any physical labour would be done by the native Africans, as the mentality was: 'For God's sake don't do it yourself, get them to do it!' Van and Goldie could not understand the pleasure derived from planting seeds in the earth and watching them grow, watering them and tending to them over weeks and months, to finally have a wonderful crop to show for all the effort. I could see Charlotte had been listening intently however, and she suddenly turned to Van and said:

"Papa, could we go to see this English garden, could we, please?" and she gazed pleadingly at her father, and carried on: "I'd like to plant some seeds, watch them grow, and help with the harvest…" I could see I'd roused at least some curiosity in Van, but his daughter seemed to thoroughly embrace the idea of my garden and was obviously very excited about it.

Van looked across at me, and then at Charlotte, finally announcing: "You name the day, and I'm sure we'd all like to come along!" to which Charlotte smiled broadly and clapped her hands in glee. I mentioned that I hadn't started anything yet, as I didn't have any tools, but Van hinted that he may be able to help. Clearly driven by Charlotte's eagerness, later that week Van managed to acquire a very sturdy garden spade for me, probably from the mine, so I could make a start. I mentioned to Fred that we may one day be entertaining Van and his family to some home cooking, made from home-grown produce, and he seemed to like the idea. But we didn't discuss the matter again, or make any firm arrangements of any sort. Maybe, like me, he suspected deep down that such a thing would never actually happen.

I waited until the worst of the rainy season was over, so my seeds didn't get completely washed away, before I very excitedly marked out a section of land right outside my bedroom window in front of our bungalow. I don't remember asking anyone's permission, perhaps I should have. No-one else had the idea anyway, that's for sure! I paced out a rectangle twelve yards by eight, and jabbed my spade into the earth for the first time. The soil was quite tough, but it was dark and rich, so it showed a great deal of promise. I spent the first day of gardening just turning the soil over, ready for cultivation, throwing my sweat everywhere, and it felt good to be doing it again. I had some very strange looks from passers-by as I toiled away, shiny-faced and glistening in just a pair of khaki shorts.

Fred shouted at me over the sound of the radio from the open window like a concerned wife: "Don't overdo it you know!" and then: "Are you going to grow some biscuits, so we can have them with our tea and coffee?" and he moved away from the window, laughing in a very dismissive, almost sarcastic manner.

"Just you wait and see!" I shouted back, confident that this little patch of African earth combined with all my sweat, efforts and knowledge would eventually produce some spectacular results. But I had no idea what I could grow, and no seeds of any sort, apart from the single paw-paw seed I'd pocketed on Sonny's picnic. Van came to my rescue yet again and came back from a trip to Bulawayo with packets of vegetable seeds. He brought them to the bungalow with Charlotte, who jumped around with joy at seeing the new garden, darting around as though her legs were on springs, jumping and leaping to and fro like a ballet dancer, or a native springbok. She was happy and in high spirits, and it was then that I really noticed for the first time just how pretty and attractive she was. She was wearing a thin cotton dress which readily revealed her slim figure, and her long legs carried her around with effortless grace.

"Dennis, can I please help with the harvest, please?" she said, as she darted around, both Van and I following her with our eyes.

"Of course!" I replied, looking at them both, "When the time comes you are all welcome to our Englander supper."

"Papa, isn't it exciting?" Charlotte said as she came to a stop at her father's side, and took hold of his left arm to give him a hug. Van looked at me with a knowing smile, before they both climbed into their car and started the engine.

"See you later, Dennis!" Van shouted from the open window of the car before driving away.

I was thrilled that I now had carrots, swedes, tomatoes, potatoes, lettuce, peas and beans. I planted them in neat rows, and watered them with a bucket from the kitchen tap in our bungalow. This was pure domestic bliss, with my own little garden heaven.

As life went on in Broken Hill I checked my garden regularly, and as the dry season progressed it needed watering at least twice a day. It was amazing to see all the seeds I'd planted eventually germinate and start to push their way up through the soil into the light. I thinned them out where necessary, then sacrificing some kite canes and string I made a basic frame arrangement for the climbing plants to attach themselves to. It was all working perfectly! I was astonished at the rate of growth my crops were making, and it was after only a relatively short time, probably six or seven weeks after planting, that I pulled up a small carrot in order to get my first taste of my African home-grown produce. It was still quite tiny but sweet and crunchy, and I was tempted to harvest more, but decided to see just how big they would become. I later noticed the paw-paw seed I'd brought back from Sonny's trip had also germinated. It seemed I could do no wrong; the conditions, and most notably the warmth, were just ideal.

My garden became the centre of passing attention, and was even mentioned in the bar where I worked. It was known that I was the Englander with the English cottage garden, and I was very proud of my achievements. I was soon offering advice on vegetable growing to anyone who wanted it, and any initial doubt or sarcasm connected to my garden was now replaced by some genuine admiration. It came as a particularly cruel blow, therefore, to find one morning, to my absolute horror, that someone, or something, had started to attack my garden during the night. I didn't notice at first, but then I saw some bean plants had whole leaves missing, and some of the tops of my carrots had gone completely. I took the necessary palliative action and after a little bit of tidying and trimming, it didn't seem too bad. But it was a real mystery, and that night I mentioned the foliage destruction to a few customers in the bar. A Scottish chap said: "Weevils! That's weevils, that is, mark my words, the damned things are everywhere!" as he sank his first beer in one enormous gulp followed by his usual whiskey chaser.

"Weevils?" I replied, genuinely curious.

"Aye, they get into everything, and you can't stop 'em

because they're everywhere. They're even in this bloody chocolate you sell behind the bar!" which was true, some of the chocolate bars sold at the club were infested with the things, but usually after a few drinks no-one noticed. He seemed very sure though, and as I served other customers some of them agreed. Once an infestation started, then you couldn't get rid of them. I tried to pump the Scot for more information, but in common with many of my customers he was drunk very quickly, and had then lost interest and inclination to talk further about my gardening problems.

The next morning I crawled around in the soil, desperately trying to spot the creatures, in the hope of perhaps removing them or isolating them in some way to prevent further crop damage. I rolled about in the dirt peering at the leaves of my bean plants, looking underneath and on the stems from the tip right down into the soil. The attacked plants showed no evidence of infestation at all, and I wondered how it was possible they were not visible, when they clearly were in the chocolate bars. Further damage had been done in the night but still there was no sign of any infestation. Drastic steps were needed, so that Friday night I decided I'd get up in the early hours in order to inspect my garden with a torch.

My alarm clock rang out with its usual, very loud clangourous racket at two o'clock in the morning. It sounded louder than ever at that time and contrary to advice I slept with my window slightly ajar so I probably woke up half of Broken Hill. I slipped on my shorts and stepped outside. There had been further damage in the few hours since I'd gone to bed. How was this possible? I examined my crops with the torch and even after close inspection I couldn't find anything. I returned to bed, a little disgruntled that I still hadn't caught any weevils.

The next night I did the same. My alarm rang out loudly at two o'clock and I raced outside to examine my plants. Still nothing. Fred was as exasperated as I was, due to the fact that my alarm was so loud it was waking him too. Again I found further damage but no weevils, or anything else for that matter. It was a real mystery.

I'd been in bed for over an hour that Sunday night when Fred came back from one of his late night canasta games. He sat in our kitchen in the dark so as not to disturb me, and was about to go to bed when he fell asleep in the chair. He woke up just after midnight, disturbed by a strange chomping noise from outside our bungalow. He immediately came into my room, sneaking around on all fours like a commando, and gently shook me awake.

"Dennis, I think you should come and see this," he said in a hushed whisper and with a wry smile on his face.

"What," I said, "What's up?"

"Just look out the window a minute," Fred said, still in a whisper, moving slowly and quietly across the kitchen floor.

There in the middle of my garden, as proud as anything, as though they owned it, stood two beautiful adult antelopes, chewing happily on the final remnants of my tattered crops.

"Oh, for God's sake…" I said, not even bothering to frighten them away at first. They were a few feet away from us and were clearly enjoying themselves and their midnight feast. Sadly Fred's camera couldn't capture the event in the dark, but it would have made a superb photograph. I turned the kitchen light on and the timid animals ran quickly and silently away.

In the morning I noticed for the first time the antelope tracks in my garden. I hadn't been looking for them before, so I hadn't spotted the signs. Weevils indeed! That afternoon I erected a fence of cane and brushwood around my little patch, which from then on offered just enough protection from my night-time marauders.

ALEC AND DIANA

Endless linear sunny days and long, warm, clear nights stretched into one and the time began to accelerate. The dry season came to an end and the rains returned in November. I suddenly realised I'd been in Africa for a full year. I mentioned this momentous event to Fred, but he simply shrugged and made little comment. We had another year in our contract yet, we were only halfway through.

I was again hugely impressed by the thunderstorms which happened during the day and often at night. In the daytime they were marked by incredibly dark blue-black clouds massing over the flat land far into the distance, the very heavy rain, and then huge beautiful rainbows which stretched right across the wide African sky. This time I noticed just how much the countryside and not just my own little garden burst into life after months of dry weather; wild flowers seemed to spring up from the earth and were everywhere; flame-red lilies, pink and yellow hibiscus, orchids and huge daisies. The air filled with their wonderful scent which would linger and drift on the warm breeze, teasing the nostrils as though we were close to a French perfumery. The many varieties of savannah grasses became green again, and the animals and birds seemed particularly lively. It was a wonderful time of year.

Fred and I had become widely known for our sober disposition, and so we were given some extra work in the form of 'sits'. This was house-sitting for mine executives, who usually took their holidays between November and March down in the Cape area of South Africa, leaving their homes unoccupied. Of course it was not difficult work; all we had to do was to live in their wonderful houses for a few weeks at a time. We were never allowed to do this together in the same house, but it was always interesting, and the money was very good. I remember on one such occasion I was living in a particularly large house which had a veranda running around the entire outside, which I had to secure every night before I went to bed. I conducted my rounds as usual and locked the front door after me and then climbed into bed. I was almost asleep when I heard footsteps outside my room and around the veranda. It sounded as though someone in bare feet was padding around the house, in and out the front door, completely at will, as though they owned the place. I was suddenly gripped by fear mixed with anger. This person had gained entry to the house somehow, and it was down to me to remove them, this was my job, it was the reason for me being there. How dare they come in without permission! I wasn't at all prepared, as I didn't have a weapon of any sort to hand, so fearing the worst I opened the bedroom door and leapt into the hallway, flicking on the light as I did so. I was sure the person was barefoot, so if I was right then it would probably be a black African trespassing in the property. The footsteps had been so close I expected to see the person right in front of me, but there was nothing. I stood momentarily rigid to the spot, looking around me. No-one was around. I checked the front door. It was locked, just as I'd left it. So was the door to the veranda. It was all secure. But I had *definitely* heard footsteps. I locked and re-locked the doors and eventually returned to my bed. I spent an uneasy night until dawn, catching short periods of light sleep, fearful of hearing the footsteps again. I remained in the house for another week but didn't have any further problems. I mentioned it in passing the next time I saw Van. He looked at me and with some seriousness in his voice said to me: "You were in the old Vorster place, is that right?"

"Yes, I think so, they were the previous occupants, they left a couple of years ago, apparently," I replied, wondering where the conversation was going, "there's a new couple in there now."

"Dennis has anyone told you about that place? They didn't leave, well, not as such," and Van looked at me and sighed. "It was bloody sad, the whole thing."

"Why, what was, what is it?" I asked, curious, scanning his expression, which seemed to change and further darken as he explained.

"He shot his wife before killing himself. So now they say the place is haunted..."

My second Christmas and New Year in Broken Hill was very memorable. I volunteered to work behind the bar at the club and on New Year's Eve we were granted a licence extension, to stay open until nine o'clock. I was assisted by two young, white Afrikaner lads who worked tremendously hard. The Afrikaner customers in the club would frequently try to converse with me in Afrikaans which at first I found very difficult to understand, particularly when inevitably their speech became increasingly slurred as the evenings progressed. Within a few weeks of working there I therefore wrote my own notice which I fixed prominently in full view for all to see at the bar, which read: 'ONLY ENGLISH TO BE SPOKEN AT THE BAR'. I doubt that I endeared myself to the Afrikaners with this sign, but if they wanted to be served then they had to ask me in English!

We opened at five o'clock on New Year's Eve, and initially I was also given some assistance in the rush by my boss, David. I could see he was occasionally helping himself to the optics in true festive spirit, and because he was probably starting from somewhere well above sober anyway, he quickly became a hindrance rather than a help. The rate of drinking was greater than on Christmas Eve and within an hour some people were incapable of standing unaided. Some of my customers were even unable to walk the necessary ten feet to the chairs provided and simply slid down the bar and sat in a heap on the floor. Clever drinkers who initially stipulated they only drank Johnnie Walker scotch were soon drinking the cheapest South African whiskey we had, and even brandy, but they never noticed, despite repeated claims of: "I know my whiskey!" The cash register began to fill up to the extent it was literally overflowing with bank notes, which then floated down one after the other like autumn leaves onto the wet and sticky floor.

The same Scotsman, Jock, who'd given me the advice about weevils, marched up to the bar with a set of bagpipes on his arm, trying his best to give us a rendition of 'Auld Lang Syne', and failing. When I refused to serve him anymore and advised him that in my opinion he'd had enough to drink, he bent down and reached into a sock. He pulled out a shiny blade like a small sword and started waving it around, mainly in my direction. The dagger glinted in the light from the bar, and even though it was probably a ceremonial item, it looked pretty fearsome to me.

"You Sassenach bastard!" he shouted, and lunged forward at the bar and tried to lift one leg as though intending to climb over. He tried this a couple times before giving up. Then to my horror he seemed to be able to stand up over the bar a lot higher than before. I realised he must have been standing on one or more of my other customers who were slumped on the floor against the bar. He crawled across the wide polished wood bar towards me, alternately dribbling and cursing as he did so. I took a step back until I couldn't move any further, and leaned against the optics, fearing the worst. Luckily, without the support of the bar underneath him, he fell forwards while grabbing at me frantically and pulling me over. My legs gave way under his weight and he collapsed on top of me, dropping the dagger and crushing the pipes between us. There was a sudden rush of air and a high pitch wheezing sound, which I'm not entirely sure was from him or his pipes, or both. I pulled myself up and left him lying on the floor for the rest of the evening. He proved to be quite useful at times too, as I could stand on parts of him occasionally in order to reach some of the higher shelves above the optics. I noticed he'd been sick all over the tartan bag of his pipes, but he was still alive, so I continued to serve the other customers, stepping over him and on him – and his pipes – on numerous occasions. This was how I saw 1952 arrive in Broken Hill.

January was again the height of the rainy season, and my adventures with Fred to the dam were restricted. Floods and mud were everywhere, making travel very difficult at times. So one Saturday we took an early morning train, free of charge of course, south for some sightseeing. We both wanted to see the Victoria Falls and decided to make it a three day trip. We'd been advised that the falls were more spectacular with a greater volume of water in January due to the rains. We passed through Chisamba and stayed the first night in Lusaka, the capital of Northern Rhodesia, mainly because neither of us had spent any time there before. It also broke up the 300 mile journey quite well. We arrived there at midday, and found a cheap hotel to stay the night. We managed to contact the Victoria Falls Hotel by telephone from there and booked the following night's accommodation.

Lusaka was clean and tidy, and was a bigger town than Broken Hill, though there wasn't that much to see. Fred and I talked at length about our first year in Africa, the prospects for 1952, and how time seemed to be flying by. Our contracts were due to expire in November, and it was then that we had to decide whether to return to the UK or stay on. We knew that many people in such circumstances often decided to stay on. But at that time such a thought never entered my head. It was always thought that I would return to the UK after two years and marry my girlfriend, Esther, and there seemed no reason to change this.

I bought more seeds for my garden, and we called in to the headquarters of Rhodesia Railways, just to say hello. It was good to meet some of the people we'd been in telephone contact with many times during the previous year, but whom we'd so far never met. They were insistent upon providing us with lunch too, which was all very civilised!

The next morning we set off early on the six-thirty train from Lusaka to Livingstone. We made good progress and we passed quickly over part of the Kafue River near Mazabuka, then through Monze, Choma, and Kalomo before arriving in Livingstone in time for lunch. We checked into the Victoria Falls Hotel and were very keen to see the falls. Astonishingly we could already see a huge cloud of mist spray rising hundreds of feet into the air, and hear a deep rumbling from the same direction. We were given instructions on how to get as close as possible to the water, and we followed a path through the trees and bushes, until the roar from the falls became a continuous thunder. Little wonder the African name for the falls is '*Tokaleya Tonga*', meaning 'The Smoke that Thunders'. The fine spray was drifting high into the warm air, gently cooling everything on contact and gathering in huge droplets on anything it touched. I couldn't believe the sheer volume of falling water that I was seeing; hundreds of yards wide and dozens of feet thick, a continuous solid mass of falling water. The noise was such that Fred and I could barely hold a conversation, so we just stood in awe staring at the sight in front of us, gradually getting soaked. I have to say that years later I stood at a similar point overlooking Niagara Falls in the USA and they were nowhere near as huge and impressive as the Victoria Falls that day.

We stood at the falls for almost thirty minutes before we came away and made our way back through the trees on the path to the hotel, utterly soaked. At that time the Victoria Falls Hotel was in dire need of modernisation. The décor and furniture looked as though it had been untouched since the place had opened at the turn of the 20th century. Of course this was where the explorer Livingstone had discovered the falls in 1855, according to a plaque in the hotel, and we joked about his later encounter with Stanley, imagining ourselves in their shoes so long ago. Without road and rail links it really would have been incredibly remote, right in the centre of southern Africa.

Sunday night at the Victoria Falls Hotel was an interesting experience. We felt as though we were in the middle of the jungle as there was a cacophony of insect and animal noises in the night, such that we'd not yet experienced at Broken Hill. We could hear baboons, elephants and lions, and it was then that Fred and I decided we must visit Mulungushi Dam in a club car and stay overnight at the dam, if we dared. In the morning we caught an early through-train to Broken Hill and apart from a brief stop in Lusaka the journey was completed in one exhausting ten-hour stretch. Our first task when we arrived back at Broken Hill was to book a car for the next available Saturday. Sadly, due to the rains, a three week wait was necessary, but then it would give us more time to prepare.

That night both Fred and I were invited to dinner at Alec and Diana's house. I'd met them both briefly on numerous occasions in the bar and on hot afternoons while lazing around the pool, but until then I'd not been to their house. I could tell Fred was extremely happy and excited at the prospect of visiting Alec and Diana, and as we walked towards their house he reminded me of the rules of canasta. I'd played a few times at Van's house, and felt quite competent, but he said our hosts were excellent card players.

The house was built on stilts, and was not a standard railway bungalow of the type Fred and I were living in. It was much larger and was similar in size to Van's house. We were greeted at the door by Diana, who was wearing a frilly and flowery white cotton dress. She was tanned, slim, and very pretty, and I could see she was wearing make-up, something I'd not noticed before. She took hold of Alec's right forearm as though about to shake his hand, but held onto it with both hands, tightly, in an obviously more familiar manner than would have been usual. I thought nothing of it at the time, as I knew Fred had been to their house on countless previous occasions. It was then left to me to shut the door behind us.

We sat down almost immediately at their dining table and were served a huge meal of steak and vegetables by two black servant boys who were helping Diana. Fred mentioned my garden and the marauding antelope and this caused quite a good humoured laugh at my expense. I spoke enthusiastically about our trips to the dam, our adventure with Sonny, and how much I was enjoying the experience of Africa. My enthusiasm wasn't reciprocated however, and both Alec and Diana simply smiled and nodded politely when listening to my stories of our adventures. When the meal was over the conversation gained a more serious tone when I asked about Alec and Diana's background. They were both quite evasive at first, as though very reluctant to bring up the subject.

"We're from the West Country originally, Devon. We met at Exeter University," Alec said, smiling and glancing at Diana. She wasn't looking at him, but down at the food on her plate. "We ran off together and got married, bloody silly really. Never told anyone until we arrived here."

I saw Fred and Diana occasionally looking at one another, stealing brief glances and quickly looking away furtively when they noticed I'd seen them. Diana spoke up: "We were promised Salisbury, but we ended up here. Do you know what I call this place, Dennis, Broken Hill? Shall I tell you? I call it 'Broken Heart'. God I hate this place. It's a prison, it's *my* prison." Diana stood up and moved over to a sideboard and poured herself a tall drink from a half-empty bottle of Johnnie Walker. She splashed a little water into the glass from a small jug and remained standing.

"There's only one thing to do here, and that's get drunk. Haven't you noticed? Of course you have, but then you don't drink do you Dennis?" She put a cigarette to her mouth and struck a match. It wasn't until then, that as she held the flame in her fingers, I noticed just how much she was trembling. She was shaking as though she'd suddenly been forced to stand in an icy blast, and I could just see the hem of her cotton dress quivering very delicately, almost imperceptibly as she stood next to me.

There was an awkward, piercing silence until Alec held out a hand across the table towards Diana and in a very peremptory tone said: "Give me one of those will you," and she picked up the cigarettes from the table and threw the packet at him, carelessly, causing it to land in the middle of his dinner plate. I felt the need to say something.

"Why don't you go home, back to England?" to which Alec sighed, then took a long pull on his cigarette.

"Because we have nothing to go back to," he replied, cigarette smoke emanating from his mouth at every word as he spoke. "We've written to both our parents countless times but we've never had a reply. It seems they just don't want to know us anymore. That's it, that's the situation. All our bridges are well and truly burnt." Diana threw Alec a withering look.

"We're trapped here," she said, taking another mouthful of scotch. Alec stood up and poured himself a whiskey.

"Trapped is a strong word, I wouldn't call it that, not quite," Alec said, standing up. "Come on, we'll go and sit down in the lounge," and he gestured with an outstretched arm for us to leave the table and follow him. "It's not as bad as all that," Alec said, looking around him. "We've got this house, some excellent bloody weather, and servants all over the place."

I smiled but felt uneasy that I'd raised the topic of conversation in the first place. Alec and I talked as we walked towards the door together, and Fred pushed his chair back under the table.

"I'll make some coffee," he said, and quickly disappeared away into the kitchen.

Diana rose to her feet. "I'll give you a hand," and followed Fred with some quick, eager steps.

I asked Alec about children, as there were clearly none in the house, to which he replied: "Can't have them, or so it seems. Probably down to me. I think she resents me for it too…" and he quickly changed the subject. He seemed very interested in our trips to the dam and then asked: "Shot anything yet, Dennis, with those rifles of yours?"

"No, not yet. Shot *at* a few things but not killed anything. Not really seen anything to shoot at, apart from baboons."

"You need to go out there at night, that's when it all comes to life, believe me. I used to shoot a lot, a hell of a lot actually," and he stood up and walked over to the corner of the room, "with this…" and produced a very smart rifle, clean and well cared for, unlike the ones we had. He offered it to me and I took it reverently in both hands. It was heavy, and felt powerful. I held it to my shoulder and looked down the sights. It had *Remington M81* written on the barrel and had a magazine underneath rather than the normal bolt action I was familiar with.

"It's American, a semi-automatic, specifically for hunting. It's a superb rifle," Alec said proudly, drawing on his cigarette,

"I bought it from a chap at the mine. You'll have to borrow it sometime." I politely declined his offer, and then to my surprise I noticed the magazine was full and there was a cartridge in the breach. It was therefore loaded, but with the safety catch in the 'on' position. I handed it back to him, carefully, and told him that Fred and I had never actually been on a formal hunt as such, but we just spent time enjoying being out in the bush.

"You must do some hunting, now that you seem to know your way around fairly well, and as I said, go when it's dark, it's better at night," Alec enthused about the numerous times he'd been shooting on overnight trips and had shot at lions and antelope, frequently bringing antelope carcasses back to make his own biltong. He told me in great detail how to reduce a whole carcass into perfect strips of biltong with a very sharp knife. I wasn't sure I'd be capable of doing it.

Fred and Diana walked in, Diana carrying a large wooden tray with four cups, some sugar, milk, and a coffee pot. She slowly and carefully poured four coffees and I told Fred about the prospect of night hunting. He nodded in a very positive acknowledgment, but he also seemed quite distracted. We drank the coffees and realised it was getting late already. The playing cards were not produced, and no-one suggested any canasta that night. I don't think the mood was appropriate.

On the way back to our bungalow Fred didn't say a word. He just let me rattle on about night shooting and making our own biltong as Alec had done. I liked Alec and Diana very much, and fully understood why Fred had grown attached to them. Diana had a subtle, understated beauty and calm, caring temperament, while Alec was the type of no-nonsense unpretentious character I could relate to.

I realised later that I had deliberately chosen to ignore the unhappy exchanges between them both that Fred and I had witnessed that evening. We all had our low points, I thought to myself. But by choosing to ignore these overt displays of unhappiness I seriously wondered whether I could have done more to help. In the meantime I would see them around

Broken Hill a lot, and sit with them by the pool on many occasions, chatting and passing the time on the warm, sunny afternoons. All the time, unknown to me, this unhappiness simmered away under the surface, waiting for the awful moment to boil over.

Fred nodded quietly as I rambled on about how much I liked our hosts as we walked back through the warm night in Broken Hill. He seemed quiet and distracted. I didn't like the way Fred had become. I asked him if he was alright and he said he was. I had no idea.

LIVINGSTONE

Two very welcome and familiar faces walked into the Broken Hill Railway Club bar that week in early 1952. Taffy and Bill had arrived and stood at my bar for several minutes before I recognised them. It had been over a year since we'd dropped them off on our first trip up from the Cape. They were lean and confident, no longer the shy, timorous individuals I knew from the boat. They were to spend the remainder of their contract at both Broken Hill and Bulawayo, so we would see a great deal more of each other. They had certainly acquired the drinking habits of the majority, as quite soon after their arrival in the bar they managed to drink a gallon of beer each and the conversation began to deteriorate. I told them of our adventures at Mulungushi Dam, and I could see they could hear me, but they were sadly not really listening.

The next day I insisted Fred take a picture of the three of us sitting at a tin table near the pool, just after I'd had a swim. Taffy was fiddling around with his camera, and somewhere in the world there must be a similar picture of me, Bill, and Fred sitting at the same table. The pool became quite a meeting place on hot days, and I was happy to see most of the people I knew gathered around it, like so many animals around a watering hole. Alec was a good swimmer, as indeed was Diana. Charlotte and her brother, Junior, were also frequent visitors to the pool, and as usual Junior had his camera with him and busied himself taking photographs of everyone present. On one such afternoon Charlotte pulled me up from where I was lying next to the water and shouted at her brother: "Take a picture of us diving in together!" and with little choice in the matter I found myself diving off the side in perfect time with Charlotte right next to me. We both reached deep water quickly, but just as I was about to swim up to the surface Charlotte swam towards me and was suddenly right in my face a few inches in front of me. Her long hair floated around her head and face like fine seaweed and to my surprise she grabbed my head with both hands and kissed me forcefully on the lips before pulling away, smiling, and swimming towards the surface, her long slender legs effortlessly propelling her upwards. I broke the surface just after her and heard her shout: "Did you get it!" to her brother. Junior replied: "Yes, I did, you both hit the water at the same time!" Charlotte laughed, and looking at me she said: "Well good, but you missed the best part!" and she climbed out the pool, smiling at me again, tossing her long wet hair down her back with a quick flick of her head. Clearly no-one else had seen the kiss deep in the water, and I was immediately shocked but pleasantly surprised by it, as any man would have been. She didn't mention it to anyone, and carried on as if nothing had happened. But things would be different between Charlotte and I from that moment on.

Saturday finally arrived again, and we collected our car. We loaded our two rifles, ammunition, fishing rods, a pair of leather gloves, three kites, string, food, water, paddles, and lashed the kayak to the roof. I noticed we had the same car and where the front of the upturned boat was in contact with the roof it had scratched the paintwork quite badly. Either no-one had noticed or they just weren't bothered. Fred was quiet and preoccupied, and still not quite himself, so to keep his mind occupied I insisted that he drive us to the dam. By the time we were under way he'd returned to his old self, and was more like the Fred I knew best. We became equally enthusiastic about our latest visit to the dam, and it seemed that we had planned to be extremely busy that weekend.

We made slow progress because the track was very muddy in parts, as we were still in the latter part of the rainy season. It was probably unwise to be attempting the journey at that time of year. We arrived later than usual at about ten-thirty, and began unloading the car. Fred handed me his camera and stood in the long grass near the car, shirt off, and posed for a photo. He'd already taken one of me earlier that day outside our bungalow, with an open shirt, hat on one side, and rifle in hand.

We left the kites and one rifle in the car, everything else we just transferred into the kayak. I threw the water bag on my back, and Fred slung a rifle on his. This was now our preferred way of equipping ourselves when venturing out in the kayak. We settled our little boat in the usual launching area, climbed in, and pushed off. We drifted for a while towards the centre of the lake and once again we were both quite speechless while gazing at the tranquil beauty of our surroundings. Fred didn't bring his camera onto the lake, but I wish he had, at least once.

Out in the middle we decided to load our fishing rods with the spinners, tossing bits of biltong over the side as bait, to see what we could catch. We needed to position ourselves back to back, so Fred leaned one way while I stood up and turned around, leaning with my weight in the other direction. It worked fine, even though the kayak did wobble slightly, and we then sat quietly preparing the lines, spinners and hooks. Fred cast his into the water and then I did the same. My reel whirred quietly, giving up the line at an alarming rate. I had forty yards of line, and just as it was reaching the end it suddenly stopped. I reeled it in slowly and could feel the lure catching the slight current as the spinner started rotating, doing its job perfectly. We both sat for what only seemed a few minutes before Fred felt a bite on his line. He reeled it in as fast as he could and eventually landed a beautiful fish, similar to a large trout, probably weighing five or six pounds or more.

"Dinner!" shouted Fred, and it did indeed look wonderful. He removed the hook and dropped the fish into a leather bag and began preparing the spinner again. The spinners seemed to be irresistible to any fish in the vicinity, and as though to confirm this I soon felt some sharp pulls on my line too.

"Got something!" I shouted to Fred, and he put his own rod onto the floor of the kayak and readied himself to give assistance. Whatever was on the end of my line was quite big, probably a ten pound fish of some sort, but I managed to reel it in successfully for several minutes until I could see the fish on the end of my line in the clear water. To my astonishment the shiny silvery fish disappeared and there was a pull on my fishing rod which almost had it completely ripped from my hands. I took hold of the reel and tried in vain to gather in some more line. Something extremely lively and very heavy had attached itself to the end of my line, and was pulling at it with such force I had to lean back against Fred to avoid being dragged overboard.

"Gloves!" I shouted to Fred, and he fumbled about frantically in the bottom of the kayak, eventually finding our tatty pair of brown leather gloves which I managed to slip onto my hands in between Fred grabbing the reel and rod together. I began to haul in the line, reeling and pulling once I'd put the gloves on, but I quickly realised that whatever it was on the other end was not in the least interested in co-operating. Our little kayak suddenly became the seat of some frenzied activity as Fred and I tried to keep our balance while at the same time we peered down into the deep water in a desperate attempt to see what was creating the problem. I wondered if the hook had caught on the bottom at first, but then it was clear that we were being pulled along through the water as opposed to simply being snagged on something immobile. I still hadn't seen exactly what was causing so much trouble and came to the conclusion that it was probably a much bigger fish intent on stealing my first catch. But then the whole thing broke the surface momentarily in front of us and there was absolutely no doubt as to what we were dealing with.

As the kayak rocked dangerously from side to side and even began to pitch forwards, the first thing I saw was a huge set of fearsome yellow teeth clamped around our fish, the tail of which was protruding from the mouth and still flapping about. I remember thinking how dirty the crocodile's teeth seemed to be, streaked with brown and not at all pearly white as I had imagined. The surface of the lake was being thrashed around as the crocodile rolled over several times trying to pull the fish from us. I tugged at the line in sharp bursts, attempting to rip the fish from the crocodile's jaws, but they were absolutely tight shut. I didn't like the way the kayak was rolling more vigorously from side to side and, judging by the expression on his face, neither did Fred. We were in the middle of the lake at the deepest point, and if this carried on much longer very soon we'd both be in the water.

There was by now some ferocious rolling and splashing from the end of my line and it was probably attracting the attention of other equally fearsome creatures in and around the lake. There seemed to be no end to the fight, which Fred and I were clearly losing. I reached down and picked up my knife. I hacked at the line a couple of times before the blade finally passed through it, and suddenly the tension was gone. The fish, together with my spinner, disappeared into the depths with the crocodile.

Calm returned to our little boat and the surface of the water, and all was quiet again. At this point I could easily have written that we'd just had our first encounter with a huge crocodile at least ten or fifteen feet long. In actual fact it wasn't very big at all. It was very small, tiny really, no more than four or five feet long. But the power it had in the water was just astonishing. It was fierce and strong, and Fred and I were immediately overcome with a huge amount of respect and admiration for the creature, and all those like them.

I managed to turn around again in the kayak; we picked up our oars and began paddling back to our launch point. I remember for some reason I started singing, perhaps to relieve the tension, I'm not sure. I'm not usually a person who spontaneously breaks out into song, but on this occasion I did. It just felt appropriate. I sang: *'Ah yee oh koe,'* over and over, then: *'the current swings, the water sings, ah yee oh koe...'* from 'The Canoe Song' by Paul Robeson. It was from the 1935 film *Sanders of the River*. How on earth I'd remembered it I've no idea. If I'd seen it at the cinema the year it was released I would have been six years old. But here I was, in Africa where the film was set, eighteen years later, paddling a canoe on a wilderness lake having just had a fight with a crocodile. Who would have believed it?

We carried the kayak near to the car and gently placed it on the ground upside down to dry. Our tangle with the crocodile didn't really frighten us as such; it just seemed to again reinforce the seriousness of where we were, as a step up from our first encounter with the baboon. It was a surprise, but then it was as though we'd somehow almost expected it. We both wanted to see such things, and they were actually beginning to happen to us, even if they were a little closer than planned. I reached into the car and took out the kites. I looked up towards baboon ridge but strangely there were none of our friends visible. We sat near the car, ate sandwiches we'd brought with us and drank fruit juice. We discussed our encounter with the crocodile, and now laughed about it, safe on dry land as we then were.

"It's definitely something to tell our grandchildren about, Dennis!" Fred laughed, and I agreed, though at twenty-three years of age I never actually imagined I'd have grandchildren, or even great grandchildren. After lunch we took both the rifles from the car and loaded them, then applied the safety catch. We each stuffed a handful of biltong under our belts, and I slapped the water bottle onto my back. I dropped a handful of cartridges into the pockets of my shorts. After securing the car, not from any thought of thieving people, but more from curious baboons, we set off. We looked and felt like seasoned African hunters, apart from the kites, of course.

Mid-afternoon up on baboon ridge that day was wonderful. It was quite cloudy but very warm, probably eighty degrees Fahrenheit, and there was a lovely breeze on the top, which made it very pleasant. I stopped for a moment to look around me at the landscape. The tall savannah grasses weaved and swayed in the breeze, like the surface of a moderate sea stretching far into the distance, with occasional small animals breaking the surface, turning, and disappearing. Baobab trees and flowering jacaranda trees were dotted around singly and in clusters, and I could see larger animals such as wildebeest, zebras and buffalo gathered around them eating and looking for shade. I wished I had some binoculars; there was so much to see, with such an abundance of wildlife. I began to set up one of the kites and was busily engaged in knotting some string when Fred whispered to me:

"Dennis…" I looked up and from nowhere a black African man, probably about thirty years of age, with two young boys appeared from the bushes and started walking up to us. His body language was passive and he wasn't carrying anything in his hands, so we didn't feel unduly threatened. I stood up and instinctively held out my right hand.

"Hello," I said, unable to tell in advance what reaction I would get in return. The man stepped up to me and took my hand and shook it in the most unconventional handshake I've ever experienced. He smiled a beautiful wide smile of perfect teeth, while the two boys with him, no older than five or six, clung to his tatty shorts, hiding behind his legs. I assumed they were his children, though I never really confirmed this. Fred pointed to the kites on the ground, and the man nodded, also pointing at them and smiling. There was no sign of the last kite we'd left behind, and so I wondered if they'd taken it and recognised these new ones. Suddenly the man shouted something in the direction of where he'd emerged, and another four little black boys appeared, running up to us laughing and giggling. I was sure these were the same ones we'd seen there before, when they were so thrilled and bemused by the sight of our kite.

I imagined the scene in their house that Saturday afternoon, a boring afternoon when his wife had probably said to him: "Why don't you take the boys up onto the ridge and see if those crazy white men are there with their kites again…"

The man shouted again and a young boy no more than about four years old slowly emerged from the bush looking incredibly doleful and sad. I then noticed he was carrying the remnants of our first kite. It was badly ripped and broken, and he was sobbing profusely. He came up to us and handed me the sorry remains of the kite. It seemed they had indeed been playing with it, to the extent that it had been used so much it had worn out, and now it wouldn't fly at all. I wanted to immediately repair it for him but decided I'd set one of the new ones airborne instead. They didn't speak any English, and I had no knowledge of their language, which was probably Shona, so communication was difficult. In Broken Hill at that time there was never any encouragement to learn the local languages; in fact they weren't even officially recognised as far as I knew. But we managed with sign language, and I drew diagrams in the ground. I indicated for one of the older lads to follow me and I handed him a new kite. I showed him how to hold it ready for a launch, into the prevailing wind. I licked a finger and demonstrated, but I'm not sure he grasped that part as he just laughed, as did the others. At the first opportune gust of wind I indicated for the lad to launch the kite skywards. Luckily it went up beautifully first time, to an ecstatic reaction from all present.

We launched the other two kites and spent the next hour giving each one in turn some kite flying lessons, until they'd mastered it themselves. I could see the man was very pleased, and seemed to be thanking us. We couldn't even tell each other our names, so Fred and I decided to call the man Livingstone. I know it wasn't very original, but it was all we could think of at the time, and the name was still on our minds from our trip to the falls. He probably did tell us his name, and those of his lads, if they were his, amongst everything else he said to us, but we most likely couldn't get our English ears around the pronunciations. I showed them how you could tie a length of stick to the end of the string and anchor it in a hedge so the kite would fly itself, and this proved the greatest development and roused the most interest, as it had when they had seen the first kite.

The sun was descending lower towards the horizon and we remembered our plan to stay out there for the night. I pulled two of the kites in and wound up the string. I indicated for the boys to keep the other kite, and I believe Livingstone thanked me again. We informed them as best we could of our intention to leave the ridge, and the boys immediately gathered around Livingstone, listening intently and with great deference to what he was saying. They then turned and started to walk away. Our parting seemed quite abrupt, but I suppose there was no point standing around too long as we didn't understand one another.

A few minutes later they were gone. I could vaguely see where they were going though, as the kite was still airborne, and it slowly eased its way down from the ridge away from the dam, catching the orange glow of the sunset occasionally until I couldn't see it any longer.

NIGHT SHOOT

We returned to the car and decided to set up our camp there. The first thing we did was light a fire because it was rapidly getting dark, and we'd seen this done in so many Western films. I don't suppose we needed a fire but Fred said he wanted to try something. He filled a tin coffee pot with water and coffee, and stood it on an arrangement of sticks and stones on the fire, just as the cowboys did in the Wild West. I lit the small petrol stove and prepared the fish. I cut and filleted our catch with no problem, as I'd done it many times before with trout back in England. I placed the fillets in the pan and they began to cook beautifully, sizzling in their own juices and sending up a beautiful aroma into the increasingly dark night. We were blissfully unaware that perhaps our cooking smells might have been attracting certain wild animals for miles around. We ate the fish on our tin plates, with bread and fruit juice. We were both very hungry and there was plenty of fish. It tasted wonderful, similar to halibut, and we ate every scrap.

After the meal we sat by the fire watching the deep red and orange flames licking and dancing around the burning logs. The fire cast an eerie, ethereal glow on Fred's face, now prominent against the black background of the night. The stars were incredibly bright and fell to the ground like a huge umbrella over our heads, touching the ground all around us. We talked and laughed about our adventures for what seemed hours, and the whole evening was a truly magical experience. But Alec was right; the night brought everything to life in the bush. Noises grew in intensity around us, and seemingly quite close.

"Shall we see what's out there?" Fred asked, standing up and moving towards the car. He reached in and found the switch for the roof light. I stood up and moved closer to the open door. Fred steered the light around, the powerful beam falling on the trees and bushes fifty yards distant.

"Bloody hell!" Fred shouted, and looked at me, then back outside. I'd never seen anything like it. There were literally dozens of pairs of eyes of all sizes reflected back in the light, moving around and staring in our direction, curious animals perhaps drawn by the cooking smells earlier or the sound of our talking. Were they baboons? Could they be antelopes? What if there were lions amongst them? I moved closer to the car and edged myself into the front seat next to Fred. I shut the door gently behind me.

"What the hell are we going to do?" I said to Fred, "They're all over the place!"

"We've got the rifles, we'll have to use them," Fred replied, revealing yet more pairs of eyes reflecting back at us in the light.

"But what would we shoot at?" I inquired, hesitantly, and with an accidental nervous squeak in my voice.

"I don't know, I suppose we could just shoot at the eyes," Fred remarked, answering, though I could tell he was as unsure and as worried as I was. He moved the light in a long slow searchlight pattern around the car. It seemed we really were completely surrounded on three sides. The only side where there were no eyes yet was the lake, but even that could change!

"We wouldn't know what we'd be shooting at," I said, quietly checking again that I'd shut my door properly while fumbling for the lock.

"Then we'll just have to stay in the car. We can't risk going out there. We don't know what we're dealing with."

I agreed, and shuffled my bottom down the seat a little, making myself more comfortable. We sat for several minutes scanning the darkness with the roof light, and all the time we seemed to be gathering more curious onlookers.

"We'd better turn out the light, Fred," I said eventually, "we don't want to run the battery down or we really will be stuck here!" and he reached down to the dashboard and threw the switch. Absolute darkness followed briefly until our eyes could adapt. Between some long breaks in the cloud a bright moon cast and eerie light around us, but there was not enough moonlight to see exactly what was watching us, marooned as we were in the car. I laughed and shook my head a little.

"What's so funny?" Fred asked with a sigh, as I could just see he was turning his head towards me.

"We came out here today to be the big white hunters," I said, "to shoot animals on our night safari, and look at us, *we're* the hunted!" and I laughed again. Fred saw the funny side to it and also laughed, but I could tell his voice was edged with some nervousness and apprehension.

"We'll be fine if we stay in the car, we'll have to sleep in here all night," he said, and he eased himself lower in his seat. The back seat was vacant, but it was covered in a scattering of the day's events, with the kites, rolls of string, food, water bag, boxes of ammunition and the rifles, all thrown randomly across it. It was too dark to see exactly where everything was, but I began to climb over the front seat.

"I'm going to get in the back, it'll give us both more room," and I heard an awful crunching sound as I realised I'd stepped on at least one of the kites. I felt around and found the rifles and ammunition. I passed the water bag to Fred and eventually managed to get quite comfortable. We sat talking for a while in the darkness, mostly in whispers for some strange reason, with the moon occasionally providing some light around the car. Then we both heard what sounded like scratching noises on the outside of the car.

"Shit!" Fred shouted, "They're trying to get in the damned car!" I looked out the window but couldn't see anything, and instinctively I clapped my hands twice as loud as I could, then the suspicious scraping noises stopped. Some tense moments passed and I looked over towards the dam. I could see the still surface of the lake reflected like a mirror in the occasional moonlight and the top of baboon ridge in a dark outline against the night sky. It all looked wonderful and peaceful, and it was probably during these restful thoughts while leaning my head on the back seat that I fell asleep.

I've no idea how long I'd been asleep when I heard someone shouting my name. I thought I was dreaming at first, and imagined I was at home in Sheffield, and none of this was happening at all. I was a child again and I was running across pit hill without a care in the world; my mum was shouting me in for dinner and I was ignoring her as usual. Then the calling was getting louder and closer, and now it was a man's voice, like my dad's, so I opened my eyes and realised Fred was leaning over me, shouting at me under his breath.

"Dennis, Dennis, are you awake, Dennis!" with some obvious urgency in his voice.

"What's up, what's wrong?" I inquired, realising that I had indeed been asleep and dreaming.

"I need a piss," he said, "sorry but I just can't wait until the morning."

"What? Can't you do it in the car somewhere?" I suggested, still almost asleep, perhaps not realising how stupid the suggestion was. But we had nothing useful to hand, no bottle or suitable receptacle of any sort. I heard a brief scuffling noise from Fred and then a short and direct answer:

"No."

I thought for a moment, waking up fully and considering the options.

"Right," I said, "you can either stick your knob out the window, which I wouldn't recommend, or get out of the car altogether."

There was silence for a moment and then: "I'll have to get out of the car," Fred replied in a subdued and slightly shaky voice. I was a little shocked at my own decisiveness, and added: "I'll keep a lookout with a rifle," as I reached down and found one of the rifles. I checked to confirm whether it was loaded, which it was, and felt for the safety catch. Fred didn't say a word and probably realised this was his only option, other than just sitting there and pissing himself. I climbed over the seats and back into the front, then reached forward and turned on the roof light. I'd never seen anything like it. It looked like the siege of Mafeking or a scene from Rorke's Drift. We were surrounded by animals of all types and they didn't seem to be afraid of us or the car. I didn't wait to see how much more of

148

an audience we could gather. I wound the side window of the car down a few minimal and tentative inches then stuck the barrel of the rifle through the gap.

"Ready?" I said to Fred, and just as I saw him nodding in the moonlight I pulled the trigger. The gun went off in the small car with such a deafening bang I think my ears are still ringing to this day. But the shattering noise certainly had the desired effect because we then heard loud screeching and barking noises all around the car, then some frantic jumping and running about through the trees and bushes nearby, followed by a few moments of silence. I scanned the surrounding area with the lamp and the curious eyes had all vanished, scattered into the bush.

"Now, Fred, do it now while they've gone!" I shouted, and he opened his door and stepped out the car. He stood immediately next to the door as close to the car as possible, and pissed against the front wheel. He must have been desperate as the dramatic rushing of liquid on the ground under obvious high pressure caused it to sound like a slightly smaller version of Victoria Falls. I fumbled about frantically, reloaded the rifle and stood guard with it at the window. For an agonising minute and a half Fred exposed himself totally to the night and watered the African earth around our beloved *Flying Eight* before he climbed back on board and slammed the door behind him.

We both managed a few hours' uncomfortable sleep folded over as we were in the car, our ears still ringing from the rifle shot, and the first hint of dawn was such a welcome sight as it streaked across the morning sky. In the hours just before sunrise it had been surprisingly cool in the car, and we were grateful of the warmth from the blankets we'd brought with us. I was desperate to stretch my legs and have a pee myself, and the first thing I did when I climbed out the car was to check our fire from the previous night. It had completely burned out, so I gathered some small sticks and kindling and set it alight again. I relieved myself in the bushes, the empty unthreatening bushes we'd been so afraid of only a few hours before. I smiled to myself. There was no conversation between us, rather like a long-married couple, unspoken but knowing, as Fred padded about outside the car preparing another pot of his cowboy coffee. My fire was doing well, and I searched around for our tin mugs. I cut the bread into rough slices and toasted it over the fire on the end of a stick. We had jam on toast for breakfast with sweet, black coffee.

Despite the fact that we'd not achieved our goal of doing some serious night hunting like the big white hunters we thought we were, we both felt a stronger connection to the place having stayed there overnight. It was a modest level of empathy that I know I felt quite deeply that particular morning, and I'm sure Fred did too. We cleared everything away and launched the kayak. We set sail again in our little boat with more biltong for bait, new spinners, rods, and a renewed appreciation of our surroundings, which looked more beautiful than ever in the very early morning just after dawn. We paddled and drifted much further down the lake than we'd ever been before. We both caught quite a large fish each, easily as big as the one we had for supper the previous night, though I was sure mine was bigger than Fred's!

We'd been on the lake for several hours without incident and were just about to turn around and head back when we saw a familiar figure on the bank to our right. It was Livingstone. I waved, and he waved back, clearly recognising us. We paddled over to him and climbed out the kayak. We shook hands again like old friends, and we showed him our fish. He seemed genuinely impressed with us, and he then bent down and drew a diagram of the lake in the dirt, as though explaining to us the various areas for good fishing and the parts to avoid. We didn't really need to be told that the day before when we'd been fishing near the mud flats we'd been in the area where the crocodiles like to feed. We also managed to understand from him that his village was not far away, and it seemed we'd travelled about a third of the way down the ten mile length of the lake from the dam. Some of the little boys ran up to us, clearly pleased to see us again. Fred and I decided right then that we would give our catch to Livingstone. He gratefully accepted both fish and wrapped them in some large leaves.

Livingstone helped push us off the beach area and we paddled back to the car, happy and content. I drove us back to Broken Hill, and we arrived just before dark.

"Shall we tell them we shot an elephant, or a lion or something?" Fred suggested.

I thought for a moment before I replied: "No. Let's not tell them anything at all."

TSETSE

We didn't discuss our expeditions other than to a select few. That night I was at Van's house, and Fred went to see Alec and Diana. I told Van and Goldie about our exploits, and after some initial laughter at our first attempted night shoot I could see that Van was quietly impressed with our determination and obvious love of his country. We played canasta until quite late, much later than I'd wanted to as I was exhausted from our trip, but I was still thriving on the euphoric energy of it all. Van's daughter Charlotte was keen to hear of our exploits and I was happy to elaborate a little in places, which seemed to cheer her up and make her smile, which in turn seemed to please Van and Goldie. I discovered Charlotte was in need of some cheer, as she was not the happiest teenager.

Two nights later when I was working in the bar a chap in a smart khaki uniform, who I'd briefly seen on a few occasions before, came up to me and addressed me by my first name.

"You're Dennis, right? You have a friend called Fred, both Englanders?" he looked straight at me with sharp, clear blue eyes.

"Yes, why?" I asked, surprised.

"My name is Mike; I work in the ranger department. Take this map, and be at this point here, you see, at ten o'clock Saturday morning, with your mate," he pushed a map across the bar, folded over where someone had drawn a pencil cross at a point probably ten miles west of Broken Hill. "You want to see Africa; we'll show it to you, right? Bring your guns." Mike didn't stay for a beer but walked out the bar straight away and was gone. I felt like I'd just had an encounter with a mysterious character from a Graham Greene novel and was a little confused but very intrigued. After work I told Fred about Mike and his map, and he was as excited as I was. In the morning we booked a car and when Saturday arrived we collected it early, eager not to be late for our bush appointment.

Neither of us had ever been west of Broken Hill. We'd heard of the Kafue River and knew that most of it was in this direction somewhere, but it was positively a 'no go' region due to the threat of Tsetse flies. These insects, similar in size to ordinary house flies, were known to carry some nasty diseases, and in particular a 'sleeping sickness' which causes lethargy, emaciation and sometimes death.

We found a rough track leading out of the town which appeared to be the one on the map. It was as bad if not worse than our track to the dam, but it was just passable. It was actually a beautiful day, though the earth was quite muddy from some brief but heavy rain in the night. It was still February, so this was to be expected. We arrived at our rendezvous point half an hour early. We sat in our car with the doors flung open, waiting patiently. Precisely on time we saw a pale green, short wheelbase Series 1 Land Rover with a canvas roof appear from an entirely different direction to where we'd come from. It pulled up sharply next to our car and two very smartly dressed uniformed white men jumped out. They were both immaculately clean, and I vaguely recognised them or someone like them from working in the bar. We shook hands and introduced ourselves.

The first said: "You can call me 'A', and this is my colleague, 'B'."

I probably looked a little curious as to why they were not prepared to give us their full names, so one of them, B, said: "We're going to look after you, don't worry, but we're taking you somewhere you shouldn't be, that's why we don't want you gossiping about who we are, right?" and he looked us both in the eye in turn.

"Yes, fine," Fred said, and I nodded. They both had very thick Afrikaans accents, and their anonymity seemed to add to the mysterious nature of events that morning. Both men were wearing sharply pressed khaki uniforms of the Afrikaner

Rangers, similar to Mike's, and they each had a pistol in a holster on their belt. They walked us over to their Land Rover and indicated for us to get in the back.

"Climb aboard gentlemen, you can leave your car here for a while, but bring your rifles, right?" and we secured the car then stepped up into the back of their vehicle, and sat on the bench seats. I knew a few Afrikaans words and I heard A say to B, who was driving: "*Uitstekend...*" meaning 'excellent', and then: "*Kom, ons gaan!*" meaning 'let's go' or similar.

The vehicle was started and thrown into gear. It bounced around on the rough track causing Fred and I to hang on tightly in the back. Our two friends chatted constantly but not in English, and laughed out loud occasionally. It occurred to me that we could be being driven into the bush for some unscrupulous reason, but then we still had our rifles with us, and they'd clearly made no attempt to take them from us. After an hour driving at a speed and in a manner that put our driving to shame, we arrived at a small remote rectangular hut with a corrugated iron roof. There was a sign outside on the wall in English and Afrikaans: 'DANGER: TSTETSE AREA!' We were led into the hut and invited to sit at a table.

"Coffee gentlemen?" said A, smiling, "No biscuits or cake I'm afraid!" and we all laughed. He lit a stove and four tin mugs were placed on the table.

"We're going to show you the *real* Africa. The boss told us about you and your trips to the Mulungushi, so it's a pleasure for us to do this."

I was curious, which 'boss' did they mean, who were they talking about?

"Who do you mean, the boss, do you mean Mike?" I asked, looking at them both. They just laughed and passed a packet of *Ateshian* Turkish cigarettes around the table. Fred and I declined but they both lit up, very soon filling the whole shed with the ubiquitous and disgusting South African tobacco fog. The water came to the boil on the stove and coffee was poured. It was strong and rich, and I loaded mine with plenty of sugar.

I asked again how they came about bringing us on this trip but they refused to say. Clearly they were not going to tell me.

After coffee, Fred and I were asked to stand outside and a few yards away from the hut. B produced a brass fumigator and promptly sprayed it down A's shorts and under his shirt, front and back. They changed hands and A did the same to B. Then it was our turn. I understood this was a necessity prior to entering the tsetse fly area. Fred and I stood to attention as though on parade while we were sprayed with the white powder under our clothing. I could feel it settling around every intimate area and orifice in my shorts.

The rangers led us through the bush for half an hour on foot. While we walked we were given some advice about shooting, the nature of the animals we were likely to encounter, when to shoot and when not to shoot. Very often it was unnecessary to fire at wild animals, and frequently it was the worst thing you could do. We were told how to correctly handle a rifle, though they were not impressed with our specimens. They were carrying superb hunting rifles, similar to that which I'd seen at Alec's place. We seemed to be heading up a slight gradient, and the bush was becoming denser as we walked. Finally we slowed, and found ourselves standing on a wide escarpment, looking down at a small lake. B stopped and turned to speak to us.

"This is a seasonal waterhole, fed by the Kafue River over there. It's almost full at the moment, as you can see…" I looked down and saw dozens, even hundreds of animals gathered around what in essence was a large muddy pond. Thick mud surrounded the water, and between them the rangers began listing the animals we were looking at. Hippos, elephants, buffalo and giraffe were the ones I immediately recognised. At the far side I saw a crocodile, then another, lying in the sun at the water's edge in the mud, motionless.

"Over there, to the right!" B said, pointing into the near distance. A pride of lions was ambling away from the water toward the shade of a single tree, probably just having been for a drink. It was an amazing sight, and the rangers were absolutely right, it was the *real* Africa.

"You should see this place in the dry season," A said, "when they're *really* thirsty, there's twice this number of animals around here!"

"Yeah, and hardly any water too, so there's quite a bit of action going on down there!" B interjected, with obvious enthusiasm. Fred and I were speechless and found a safe place to sit on some rocks, with a grand view of the waterhole. Our hosts remained standing, constantly looking around, talking between them in Afrikaans. I took a sip of water and handed the water bag to Fred.

"I could stay here all day," Fred remarked.

"Me too," I replied. "I'd like to get closer," I said, "but I don't suppose we can. It's probably not safe," and I looked at our two ranger friends deep in conversation.

"Don't get any ideas, Dennis," Fred looked seriously at me, "this is as close as we're getting!"

We stayed observing our own personal zoo for about twenty minutes or so before the rangers indicated we should leave. It was probably beyond midday – I never wore a watch – and we had to get back. As we walked back towards their hut, the rangers occasionally stopped and showed us what, to me, appeared to be simple scuff marks in the ground, but were apparently lion tracks. I could then see the pad marks in the soil, quite clearly those of a large cat. It was fantastic to be given this personal tuition in bush craft and both Fred and I lapped it up wholeheartedly.

We arrived back at the hut and were given more coffee. We talked about what we'd seen and thanked them profusely. I think they realised how grateful we were. Then we climbed back aboard their Land Rover for the hour's drive to the place where we'd left our car. When we reached it the rangers showed us to our car before shaking hands with us again.

"Put what you've been wearing today straight to wash when you get back, and make sure you take a shower. It was nice meeting you blokes," and both our guides climbed into their vehicle. B leaned his head out of the window and shouted: "We never met, right, and you've never been here!" They waited until we'd successfully started our car and had set off before they disappeared into the bush.

We set off and followed the track east in the direction of Broken Hill. Fred was driving the car in a quietly confident manner. I watched him as he held the steering wheel tightly with both hands, occasionally cursing when the ruts and mud in the track tried to tear it from his grip. His expression changed constantly to match the terrain, from deep concern to obvious relief when another rough patch was successfully covered. There were beads of sweat on his forehead which would occasionally gather together, forming droplets which rolled down his face, which he'd often try to blow away, pursing his lips then huffing and puffing as though blowing out candles on a birthday cake. Then he'd smile broadly and turn his head, catching a glimpse of me looking at him. He was clearly enjoying himself.

After half an hour I suggested we pull over. Broken Hill wasn't far away but I needed to stretch my legs. The *Flying Eight* was not the most comfortable mode of transport. We stopped in a relatively flat area of ground near some thorn bushes and acacia trees. Tall grass bordered and defined the track and I stood by the car gazing across the endless savannah. Fred had lifted the bonnet of the car for some reason, and was leaning over, tinkering with the engine. I know he probably had no idea what he was looking at.

"Is everything alright?" I asked, idly, not really taking my eyes from the distant plain in front of me.

"Yes, just having a look," he replied, and then I saw him slowly stand upright and turn towards me, and then back along the track. I think he was intending to tell me, but I'd seen them already. A large herd of elephants appeared from behind the trees and slowly meandered across the track fifty yards in front of the car. *Not a problem,* I thought, as we'd encountered similar when on one of our first cycling expeditions. We just stood there by the car, quiet and still, watching them tramp across the muddy road, heavily but elegantly, little ones in front urged on behind by the adults. Luckily and much to our relief they paid us no attention at all. The adult elephants were just enormous, huge solid grey beasts, some with prominent white tusks which seemed four or five feet in length. I tried counting them as they passed but I lost count after twenty. Some stopped and moved around the others, and it wasn't until the large adults had cleared the path that we realised there were some young ones still standing in the track in front of us.

Three of the youngsters stood there, unlike their parents they seemed to be looking at us, perhaps curious at seeing a car, and people, for the first time. Fred and I stood staring at the young elephants, and they stared back, as though in competition with us. Five minutes passed, and then ten and still they didn't move. The rest of the herd were not far away, as we could hear the breaking of trees and we could see the adults now a hundred yards or so to our left. Fred lifted the cowling over the engine and deliberately dropped it with a bang onto the car. Still they didn't move. There was no way around them so we had to get them off the track, somehow.

I looked around under an acacia tree and found some sticks and started waving one of them around above my head. No reaction. I stepped a few yards closer to them, constantly checking to see where the adults were. I heard myself shouting at the little elephants: "Shoo!" and they just looked at me as though I was a lunatic. I waved my stick again in vain, and probably in exasperation I threw it at them, thinking we might need to get a rifle and fire a shot in the air. The stick struck one of them on the back, causing no injury of any sort, but it was enough to startle the little beast, and he began walking away in the direction of the herd. Thankfully the others followed. With the track now clear, we climbed back into the *Flying Eight* and drove back to Broken Hill.

FIRST KILL

I didn't work in the bar every night, and on the occasions when I wasn't working, I still went there sometimes and sat with a Coke, or an Oros fruit juice, looking and feeling completely sober and incongruous among the heavy drinkers. Fred and I seemed to be the only teetotallers in Broken Hill, certainly amongst the men, but I did notice quite a few wives frequented the bar, though not quite every night. Even when Fred was not in the club with me I was never lacking in company due to the fact that all the other customers saw me as a familiar face and obviously knew me, or at least thought they did.

I had further discussions with Roy Welensky about the Empire – the British still had one at the time – and the future of Africa. I told him of our trips to the dam, and our meetings with Livingstone and his boys. He sat opposite me, completely filling his chair, his red braces stretching to the full across his shirt, as he leaned forward looking around him almost furtively.

"You shouldn't discuss your relationship with the natives in here, or anywhere else for that matter, Dennis," and he looked very serious.

"Why, what's the problem?" I asked, already aware to some extent that close encounters with the Africans was frowned upon, other than on a strictly work-related basis.

"I'm just saying it could get you into trouble. You might be ostracised, at the very least. Just be careful," he said, and continued: "Don't misunderstand me, I'm more sympathetic to the Africans than you might imagine. You know how most of them are treated; you see it all the time. I don't think this situation can go on forever. The world is beginning to change."

I took a sip of my Coke and he lit a huge cigar, and then swilled his brandy around in his glass. Cigar smoke rose in great clouds, adding to the already smoke-filled atmosphere. The

159

drinkers in the club seemed to match the vast amount they drank directly with their smoking. By the end of the night the room was so full of the awful thick tobacco smog that you could cut your way through it with a pair of scissors. Roy always seemed to wear the same red braces over his shirt, never a belt, and he tugged at one of them slightly before carrying on:

"One day, probably not in my lifetime, there could even be complete self-governance by the Africans here. I know it sounds ridiculous, but look what's happening just over the border in the Congo, you've seen it, I know you have," and he took another long pull on his cigar. "The natives are getting restless, Dennis, we need to recognise this, or we could find ourselves with our own bloody Mau Mau right here." Roy was referring to the armed insurrection in Kenya against British rule which seemed to be gathering strength at that time despite some harsh, even brutal repression. He told me he advocated some power sharing with the black Africans in a new state, a Federation, but which would remain a British colony. This was a radical plan but he told me it was gathering strength, though it was understandably being met with some tough opposition, mainly from the white Afrikaners. These were very complex topics and I enjoyed our political conversations, but he warned me again to be careful who I discussed such matters with.

The ranger, Mike, was a very interesting character too, and he came into the bar on several occasions and sat quietly with a beer. I spoke to him whenever I could, keen to extract more information from him about the bush, the native animals and so on. I think he found our continuing amateur exploits to the dam quite amusing, but he was always happy to offer advice. He smiled when I told him how much we had enjoyed our trip west with the two rangers, but he continued to be reticent about us breaching the tsetse fly restricted area, so I didn't pursue it. As a Ranger he had a professional, pragmatic working relationship with nature, and told me he didn't advocate the random killing of animals, far from it, he had enough trouble with poachers. But he also told me that part of his job was to help correctly manage the wild animals, and so

160

he was not overly sentimental about them. He told me we ought to exchange our single shot rifles at the armoury for semi-automatics, just in case. Single shot rifles were perfectly alright under normal circumstances, but in an emergency we should be ready for anything.

"A charging hippo might be a difficult target, Dennis," he said, with a very serious tone in his strong Afrikaans accent, "and could take more than one shot to bring down." To which I nodded in agreement, bowing to his superior wisdom on the matter.

I remember the night I told Fred about this particular piece of advice when I returned to our bungalow, but he didn't seem very interested, and left in a hurry, saying he had promised to help Diana at their house. I found out later that Alec was away for a few days, in Salisbury for a job interview. Diana was apparently thrilled at the possibility of leaving Broken Hill at last.

I continued to practice my diving in the pool, trying to perfect a swallow dive and a somersault. The swallow dive in particular seemed to extend the flight through the air and I was beginning to fine tune it to perfection. Taffy was a keen swimmer, more so than Fred, and we had a great time competing for the best dive. Try as I might I could not get the hang of using the spring board, and almost always mistimed the bounce, sending my knees virtually up into my chin on some occasions. I don't think I have ever been as physically fit as I was in those days though. We were all lean and tanned, and I have a photograph that Fred took near the pool of Taffy holding me by the shoulders as I balanced on his knees, my legs straight in the air, like a pair of super-fit gymnasts.

Another Saturday came and Fred and I loaded the car. I'd been thinking of Mike's advice so we drove across to the armoury. Without a great deal of questioning we were given semi-automatic rifles as a straight swap for our bolt-action ones, and a large box of ammunition. I was given some rudimentary instructions on its use, but I had fired similar when I'd been in the army. I noticed both our new rifles were similar if not the same as the one Alec had shown me at his house; powerful and more than fit for purpose.

We drove straight to the dam early and parked in our usual spot near the kayak launching area. I'd brought along a few cans and bottles for target practice with our new rifles, and I lined them up on the ground facing the open bush land. I filled the magazine with ten rounds, placed the targets about thirty yards away and cocked the rifle. I was astonished at the power of the weapon, which would keep firing as fast as I could pull the trigger until all the ammunition was gone. The rapid fire shattered the silence at the dam, and then again when Fred fired his rifle. But after several practices we were both hitting the cans every time.

Though we'd brought along the kayak as usual, we decided to head up to baboon ridge first with a new kite, a bigger version, in case Livingstone and his troupe of boys were there. As we arrived at the top there was no sign of anyone and no wildlife either: not surprising really after the noise we'd been making. None of our friends, the baboons, were there, and it seemed very quiet. It was a beautiful clear day in the dry season, and as usual there was a refreshing, gentle breeze at the top of the ridge. We launched the kite and sent it high up into the blue, and then we anchored it in a hedge and sat down. We both must have looked quite odd, two grown men flying their kite, each with a powerful rifle slung across our backs. Fred wasn't particularly talkative and seemed quiet and distracted. We lazed around on the grass and shared some biltong and drank water.

Suddenly Livingstone arrived, probably having seen the kite, looking very anxious and babbling away at us in Shona, which neither of us could understand. He ignored the kite and kept repeating: *"Chikona! Chikona! Bwana!"* but Fred and I were clueless as to what he meant. Livingstone then started gesticulating for us to go with him along the ridge, so we left the kite tied to the bush and followed him. After about half a mile or more we heard loud bleating noises, like a distressed sheep, and Livingstone then started to slow to a walking pace.

He held out an arm and crouched down, indicating for us to do the same. Livingstone then turned and whispered to us again: *"Chikona, bwana!"* and pointed to where the noise was coming from. Fred and I peered through the long grass and still couldn't see anything, but we heard the sounds of an animal clearly in some distress. Livingstone seemed worried and was looking around him constantly. Finally I saw a large black sable antelope and then a smaller dark brown one standing close to it, most likely a female sable, both seemingly unable to move.

I then realised that each of the sable had one leg caught in a metal trap. I edged closer and could see the trapped legs were in a terrible state and had been ripped down to the bone. The beautiful animals must have been in tremendous pain. I wondered why Livingstone hadn't dispatched them himself, but then he made a shooting movement with his hands, as though asking us to do it for him. I was glad we'd not walked in the vicinity before, and was unaware that such traps had been left lying around. It would probably not be enough to cripple a man, but it would still be very unpleasant if stepped on by accident. Fred and I looked at each other, and then at Livingstone. He was looking at us expectantly, as though waiting for us to do it, and sure that we would do it.

"This is it, Fred," I said, "our first kill, we have to do this…"

"You can do it, Dennis, you're a better shot than me," Fred replied, even though he was taking his rifle from his back in readiness.

"If we have to do it, we'll do it together," I said, looking at Livingstone and checking my rifle was loaded, "we'll shoot one each, aim for the head if you can, a good clean kill." To this day I wondered if the chance to shoot the sable was given to us by Livingstone as a gift, perhaps in the knowledge that we were looking for just such an opportunity. At first I thought the traps were his, but I later found out that such things were laid by black poachers, quite careless and irresponsible as to who or what would step on them. I thought of Livingstone's boys and cursed under my breath at how dangerous they were.

The trapped animals were in possession of some sharp pointed horns protruding from their heads, and were quite large, so it may have been difficult and dangerous to grab hold of them. This didn't occur to me at the time, I was full of 'big white hunter' bravado, and was preparing myself for a first kill. From about twenty yards, almost the same distance as the firing squad training, we both took aim.

"Wait until they are still, and then take aim. The head is best for a quick kill, aim for the head," I said, giving instructions to Fred, as though I knew what I was doing, "and fire at least a couple of times, to make sure…"

"On three," I said to Fred, "ready?" We cocked our rifles. "Ready."

"One, two," then just as I said the word, both rifles rang out in an almost perfect synchronised shot, followed immediately by another, and one more each, in quick succession. The animals were immediately knocked to the ground and were motionless: dead in an instant.

Livingstone ran up to the animals and prized open the fearsome steel jaws of the traps with the help of two older boys, then from nowhere he pulled out a length of rope and began lashing them together. A small crowd of other boys were pushing and shoving each other to get a good view of the proceedings. Within a few short minutes both animals were trussed up tightly and were being dragged through the bush in the direction of Livingstone's village. The boys were chattering and laughing, helping Livingstone drag the weighty beasts behind them. Fresh blood, thick and deep red, spattered the dry earth, and there was a unique and distinctly sweet aroma of recent death in the air, carried on the warm breeze. No doubt the pungent odour of the kill could well have carried far away, arousing the interest of other, less friendly animals.

Livingstone paused and looked back at us; the rope taught in both hands over his right shoulder, and as though correcting himself after suddenly remembering we were there, said: "*Tatenda, bwana, tatenda!*" which I guessed correctly as meaning 'thank you', then indicated for us to follow him. It seemed the natural thing to do, so Fred and I slung our rifles on our backs and walked with Livingstone along the track, following the boys and the meat as it was dragged slithering through the bush.

It wasn't far to the village, and I was surprised just how close it was. I realised then that the kites would have been clearly visible to them on that first day, and the gunshots would have seemed very close, and were probably worrying to them. There were around half a dozen small round huts that I could see, with off white walls and thatched sloping roofs. It was a smaller village than the one I'd intruded into months before when on my police duties. The difference in atmosphere to that incident could not have been greater.

It seemed the whole village turned out to greet us, happy and jubilant, and I could see one of our kites parked in a tree nearby, hanging delicately, in pride of place. Everyone wanted to shake our hands, and we were made extremely welcome. There was frenzied activity around the sable carcasses, and huge excitement. I saw strips of meat hanging from a tree in the sun obviously drying out, and we were ushered into one of the huts, presumably Livingstone's home. To my surprise the inside was incredibly clean and tidy, as though perhaps I expected it to be otherwise, for some reason. It was far more spacious than I imagined too, and we were instructed to sit down on a wooden bench and then offered a cup of liquid which appeared to be fruit juice. I took a small sip, and it was indeed juice of some kind, probably mango. It was quite thick, with bits in it, but it was very sweet and refreshing.

It was such a shame we couldn't communicate, but when human beings are on good terms, words are not always essential to express friendship and empathy. Our wooden cups were refilled and I noticed that these cups were probably hand carved, so I pointed this out to Fred. Livingstone was quite astute because he saw this, and reached down, holding up the most exquisite wood carvings of African animals. He showed me how he did it, from solid lumps of wood, with a knife and a curved piece of glass, it was quite extraordinary.

The house filled with children and laughing women, and was a busy bustling place. After a while we indicated to Livingstone that we had to go, and stood up. He gestured for us to stay but we stepped over to the door. He gave us a large handful of fresh biltong, obviously homemade, and we said our goodbyes. Livingstone then came up close to me and said: "*Bwana, shamwari bwana,*" which sadly I didn't understand at the time, but later I realised '*shamwari*' meant 'friend'.

We walked back up towards the ridge, avoiding the area where the traps were, and waved to the village children as we made our way into the bush and out of sight. We retrieved our kite, which was still motionless fifty feet in the air, and returned to the car for lunch. We ate our boiled egg sandwiches that Fred had made that morning, with some of Livingstone's delicious biltong, and then set off on the lake in our kayak.

We had no agenda other than to perhaps paddle for a while to see where we would end up. It was as beautiful and serene as always, and we began to feel like part of the African landscape. We passed baboon ridge, then the mud flats, and reached the furthest point we'd ever been, but just carried on going. After a while we both spotted a beach area on the left, and Fred suggested we land the kayak for a break. We'd not been on the western side of the dam before, so we dragged the kayak out of the water and decided to explore a little. Rifles, water bag and biltong under our belts, we set off.

Fred led the way as we climbed higher above the lake through the trees, glancing back occasionally to remember where we were. There were animal tracks we could follow, regular routes trampled through the bush, providing us with navigable paths to the top of the hill. It was strange to see Mulungushi Dam from this new angle, and we took a sip of water to savour the view and celebrate another first. In front of us was the water, and behind there stretched miles of open savannah. We walked along the edge of the ridge for a while, astonished at the view on either side of us.

We were quiet, hardly speaking, reverently taking in the view, when we both sensed the approach of something with a very heavy footfall. There was a definite resounding vibration in the earth with the sound of some weighty feet, and they were getting nearer. Suddenly a huge black animal with a curly horn down each side of its head appeared from behind some trees and seemed to be walking briskly towards us, parting the tall grass in front as it did so.

"Buffalo!" Fred shouted to me in an obviously surprised and excited tone, and I turned and saw that it was gathering speed and coming straight towards us. Whether it was simply aggressive, or perhaps protecting its young, I'll never know, but it seemed fully intent on getting to us and trampling all over us. We'd seen buffalo of this sort at watering holes when we passed them on the train, but it wasn't until then that I realised just how big the beasts were.

"Fred, we've got no choice…" I said, perhaps with some trepidation in my voice.

"I know Dennis, it's not stopping," Fred replied, quickly taking his rifle from his shoulder. A shot in the air may have done the trick and frightened the animal away, but it was getting so close as to be too late, it was almost upon us. We didn't wait, we really had no choice. Fred fired first, and then I aimed straight at its huge head. We each fired at the colossal beast several times, but it still kept on coming towards us. In this instance a single shot rifle would have been virtually useless. Birds scattered into the air from the trees all around us and I took steps back and to the side away from its path and was aware that if I tripped and fell I'd probably have a ton of buffalo on top of me.

I fired at it again and the huge animal thundered past us just at the point we'd been standing only moments before. It seemed to lose its footing and then it plunged, as though in slow motion, straight over the edge of the ridge. I heard it tumbling down the slope towards the lake, crashing loudly through the bushes and bouncing off the trees until it finally fell silent at the bottom. Fred and I leaned down towards the water. The buffalo was at the water's edge, a few hundred yards from our kayak. I thought it was dead but then it appeared to move, as though trying to stand. It was clearly injured.

"We need to shoot it again," I said to Fred, and he agreed. I could feel my heart pounding in my chest, and almost up in my throat. We stood on the ridge and aimed down at the injured animal. Another few shots each from our rifles rang out across the water, echoing back at us from the other side. From what could have been almost a hundred yards it seemed we both hit the target. The buffalo stopped moving.

"Are you alright, Dennis?" Fred enquired, looking at me inquisitively. I could see my hands were shaking, whether trembling from the thrill of the kill or from just having to shoot an otherwise healthy animal, I wasn't sure.

"I'm fine, thanks," I replied, "just a lot of excitement," and I could see Fred was also a little shook up. "Let's get back to the kayak and head home," I said, and we started walking back along the ridge. I ripped a piece of biltong from my belt and offered some to Fred.

"Two kills in one day!" Fred exclaimed, starting to chew, "Who would have believed it!"

"Three altogether!" I exclaimed, hardly believing it myself.

Twenty minutes later we were climbing into our kayak. As we did so I noticed the carcass of the buffalo in the near distance had already attracted some attention. I counted at least five crocodiles around it, one or two with their jaws clamped around a limb, trying to rip it apart.

Our flimsy kayak was gliding over the water, smoothly and expertly propelled along by two great white hunters. Under the surface there must have been more crocodiles. We paddled carefully but quickly all the way back up the lake to the car.

THE PIANO

I continued to visit Van and his family regularly, and grew to know them all very well. It seemed Fred had his dinner parties and canasta evenings mainly with Alec and Diana, and I had mine with Van and Goldie. There were some occasions when the two of us attended both houses, but these were quite rare. As the months passed in 1952, I began to realise that I was becoming the subject of yet more cheerful and playful flirtations from Charlotte, and while I wasn't aware of consciously encouraging this, perhaps I should have been more active in curbing it.

I remember one evening I was at the Mine Club, on the first of quite a few such visits in company with Van and his family. The mine area and all the buildings had a strange odour that no-one was willing or able to explain, but everyone was aware of. It was a bad smell that pervaded everything and clung to the clothing. The bar at the mine was similar to the Broken Hill Railway Club and I walked down a dark corridor looking for the gent's toilet. As I did so I noticed a door on my left which was open and revealed a small store room with packing crates and heaving bags everywhere. At the back near the window in the light from the open doorway I could see the vague outline of an upright piano covered over in a huge off-white dust sheet. I walked over to it, took hold of one side of the sheet and pulled at it slowly to fully reveal the piano. Thick dust which had accumulated over many years hung in the still air from the sheet, and I dropped it to the floor. I dragged some boxes around and found one strong enough to use as a piano stool so I heaved it across the wooden floor. I didn't turn on the light but left the door wide open, then sat down quietly and opened the lid. The keys were in perfect condition.

I'd had some occasional piano tuition when I was a child, and was progressing quite well until the lessons sadly came to an abrupt halt when my piano teacher's house took a direct hit from a German bomb in November 1941 during the Blitz. She lived a halfpenny tram ride away on Granville Road, which was a little closer to the centre of Sheffield. My teacher was fine, having luckily sought refuge in her Anderson's shelter in the garden, though she was understandably very upset and traumatised at having lost everything in an instant. Concerned neighbours continued to find scattered remains of her possessions, including parts of her beloved piano, for days afterwards, with the black and white keys having been thrown in all directions from the force of the blast for hundreds of yards around. Children collected them with great enthusiasm until almost all eighty-eight were returned to her where she now lived with a neighbour. A nice gesture, but one which probably upset her even more. I'll never forget my first visit after the bomb had struck. I stood on the edge of a huge precipitous hole in the ground where her house had once been, forlornly clutching my little music bag, completely aghast at the sight before me. She was a relatively young woman at the time and as far as I know she joined the WAAF: the Women's Auxiliary Air Force. She never returned.

So it was that I could play some rudimentary tunes and had managed to find the notes for some parts of famous classical pieces, but in no way would I ever have said that I could play the piano. What I did play was entirely for my own amusement, and was not intended for public performance. I gazed with pleasure and anticipation at the very old piano in front of me and tried to recall something to play. No-one was around, so I placed my fingers on the keys and began to touch a few notes, softly at first, until I relaxed and began to play a little louder. The piano was quite out of tune, but the tone was good, and the sound was wonderful. The pedals worked, and I played the few bars I knew of Debussy's 'Clair de Lune', some of the *adagio* from Mahler's '5th Symphony', and then some of Tchaikovsky's '5th Symphony'. I played with one finger of each hand as best I could, initially making frequent mistakes, but I thoroughly enjoyed it. I was totally absorbed in what I was doing and after a few minutes I began to sense someone else in the room. I turned and saw Charlotte standing at the open doorway looking slim and curvy, silhouetted against the light.

"Dennis that was beautiful," she said, as she started walking over to me. She looked very pretty and seemed surprised to find me sitting at a piano and apparently playing it. She then said: "Teach me to play, will you, please?" as she stood closer to the piano.

"I don't really play you know, so I can't teach you…" but I could see she wasn't listening to me.

"Play it again, please," she said, and leaned on the top of the piano, gazing at the keys and then at me. I played my short repertoire, one piece after the other, all the time aware I was being stared at very intently. When I stopped playing she clapped loudly and smiled, saying: "Come on, I want to tell *everyone* about your piano playing!" and she took my hand and pulled me away, into the corridor and back towards the club. She bounced up to her parents, skipping and dancing as she walked, then proudly announced that not only could I play the piano, but that I would also teach her to play. She was suddenly exuberant, much more than I'd ever seen her before, and she jumped around on her toes as though she'd just been told it was Christmas and her birthday all in one.

This news of the piano obviously came as a complete shock to Van and Goldie, who looked at me inquisitively before Van said: "A piano player, Dennis? You never told us about this." I tried to explain, but Charlotte was so clearly thrilled by the events that I could see they didn't want to spoil the mood. I saw Van and Goldie looking at one another and then at Charlotte, and I could tell they were surprised and very pleased for her. I'd often thought that she was frequently very quiet and introspective, too much so for a girl of her age, and I later found out this was due to a diagnosis of real depression. To see her suddenly behaving like this was a wonderful sight for her parents. It seemed I was becoming the catalyst for many of her good moods, and she was now behaving in the same

171

manner as on the occasions when she spoke about my little garden. The discovery of the piano and the possibility of being taught to play even rudimentary tunes seemed to energise her completely.

"Well, we'll have to see about it, won't we," Van said to her, looking at me and smiling. I was dragged back into the store room to play what I could for Van and Goldie, while Charlotte literally jumped around with glee. She begged Van to agree to her request and I could hear him finally relenting, obviously in order to pacify her. The piano was old, out of tune, dusty, and in the mine club. Lessons were therefore out of the question. I knew it and so, I suspect, did Van.

Several days passed and Fred asked me about another trip to the dam. We agreed to book a car for the next weekend. After work in the club that night Van made sure he found me and spoke to me with some peremptory seriousness in his voice.

"Come home tonight, Dennis, you must come to supper, we have a surprise for you!" he said before he left, smiling, shouting back: "Don't be late!"

I was curious about his use of the word 'home', as though I was such a frequent visitor his house had indeed become my home. I wondered if my relationship with Van and his family had become too close, and in particular my increasingly close attachment to Charlotte. But what else could I do? The relentless sun-drenched days and sultry blood-warm nights seemed to conspire together to create the unique romance of Africa, an irresistible and beguiling force which overpowered the rational mind and subjugated all common sense. I perhaps knew, somewhere in the back of my mind, that I was heading for disaster, but found it all too captivating to let go.

Just after seven o'clock I arrived, to be greeted at the door by Charlotte as usual, who shouted:

"Dennis is here!" loud enough for all to hear. I was then literally dragged across the hallway and up the stairs to an empty bedroom at the back of the house, dark but partially lit by a full moon from the huge window. Bathed in the white ethereal glow of moonlight was the piano from the mine club. It had obviously been cleaned and restored, the polished wood and the keys reflecting some of the glow from the window. Van and Goldie had followed us up the stairs and stood in the doorway. Van switched on the light and I moved over to the piano. A stool had been found from somewhere, and so I sat down.

Van said: "Charlotte is a different person, Dennis, since you got to know her, even more so since you found the piano. It would be great if you could teach her to play something, anything…" he said, and both he and Goldie were smiling broadly. I could just see tears forming in Goldie's eyes, like ice melting in bright sunlight.

"Of course," I said "I'll do what I can," I replied, shocked at the speed of events, and still unsure as to what I could do. Clearly they were impressed with the little knowledge that I had, but if it made Charlotte happy, I had to try.

Charlotte threw her arms around Van saying: "Papa, thank you, it's wonderful!" as she moved up to the piano and sat next to me.

"We'll leave you to it then," Van said, stepping away from the doorway.

"Supper will be ready soon, I'll shout you," Goldie said, as they both left the room. My first appointment as unpaid piano teacher began with 'Clair de Lune'. I played it slowly, extracting everything I could from the pauses between notes, and when I'd finished I explained the tune was about moonlight. Charlotte jumped up and turned off the light, and the pure white moonlight filled the room again. I played it several times, with my right hand, and began showing Charlotte where to place her fingers, on the B flat and D flat keys. She certainly had pianist's fingers, long and slender with a good reach across the keys. *At least this aspect of it wouldn't be a problem*, I thought to myself, as I held her hand, guiding it over the keys. She reciprocated her movement with my hand, her fingers moving perfectly in time with mine, her breathing warm and close next to me, and after a short time wherever I moved she followed, as though we'd been moulded into one. We were in tune, together, drifting and falling into the music, connected utterly to each other and to the piano perfectly.

I heard Goldie shouting from downstairs and suddenly the spell was broken. For a few strange minutes I'd been far away, drenched as we were in the moonlight and completely transfixed by the movement of our hands on the keys.

"Play something else, Dennis, please!" she whispered affectionately, close to my ear, taking hold of my right hand and squeezing it tightly.

"But we have to go, your mother…" I tried to speak but she looked at me, warm and wide-eyed.

"Please, let's not go yet, please play something else!" She said as she moved my hand onto the keys firmly, insistent and determined. I gently moved my fingers over the keys and very slowly part of the *adagio* from Mahler's '5th Symphony' emerged, haunting and beautiful. I could see Charlotte's eyes began to water, and in a glance I could see they were shining silver in the moonlight. Again I was lost in the moment, and just as her face was close to mine she kissed me and I reciprocated, her hands gripping mine tightly on the keys in front of us.

I finished playing and stood up. Charlotte led the way towards the stairs, and we passed a door marked on the outside with handwritten notices: 'PRIVATE – NO ENTRY TO ANYONE', and 'KEEP OUT'. Charlotte saw me looking and heaved at my arm.

"That's MY room. You are not to go there, ever!" she shouted, whether serious or not, I couldn't tell. I didn't give it another thought. Downstairs we sat at their dining table and Charlotte's brother, Junior, immediately asked me about the music.

"That last piece I heard you play, it sounded very sad, why would you want to play music that's so sad?" he said, looking quite intently at me.

I wasn't sure what to say, but replied: "It doesn't have to be sad," I said, "it can be relaxing and reflective, you might understand this when you get a bit older. I'm sure you'll hear it a lot more once your sister knows how to play it," and he laughed. At the dinner table I noticed every time I looked at Charlotte she was staring at me. Or maybe it was just that I couldn't help but stare at her? I felt emotional turmoil, a mixture of increasing excitement and yet some nagging trepidation. I told Junior about our kite flying and promised one day I'd bring a kite round to the house and show him how to fly it.

When the meal was finished, the five of us played canasta for several hours. Charlotte was paired with me, and to her delight we eventually won. She held onto my hand during most of the evening, even in the absence of a piano. I was falling into something head first and with both eyes wide open.

I returned to our bungalow at midnight, walking very contentedly through the warm familiar moonlit paths and roads of Broken Hill.

THE ENVELOPE

At the end of August 1952, the countryside around Broken Hill and the wider savannah of Northern Rhodesia was tinder dry. It hadn't rained for more than three months, and when we arrived at the dam we could tell for the first time that the water level was lower than normal. The mud flats were much wider, and we were very conscious about whether we should light a fire. As we pulled up at our usual parking spot we found it had been taken, not by another vehicle but by quite a few elephants. They had clearly been down to the water for a drink, and were already moving away. I remembered what the rangers had said about the dry season and the popularity of water holes. I don't remember noticing any of this in my first year at Broken Hill, but now these things all seemed to fit into place, and were part of the rich patina of life in rural Africa. Fred was driving the car, so I jumped out and clapped my hands loudly, which was enough to move the animals on. Neither of us thought to reach for our rifles.

There was an unspoken, sombre mood between us when Fred and I took the kayak from the roof of the car in our now very practised and familiar routine. We loaded it with the usual fishing supplies, bait, water and biltong. I think we both realised there was a strong possibility, with the rainy season fast approaching, that this could feasibly be our last trip together to the dam. We were both due to return to England in November. The thought of leaving Africa filled me with trepidation, perhaps as much as when I sat alone on the platform at Waterloo almost two years before.

We pushed off and drifted slowly out onto the lake. Fred started to prepare a spinner and a hundred yards from the bank I decided to turn around in the kayak, forgetting to warn Fred. I realised too late that far too much weight had fallen onto one side of the kayak, and to my absolute horror I could sense imminent and irreversible disaster. Curiously I felt a solid bump underneath the kayak just at that moment and it very suddenly flipped over completely and capsized, throwing me into the water with a loud splash. At least I was momentarily prepared, but Fred was turned and thrown into the lake utterly oblivious. I surfaced immediately and looked around but there was no sign of Fred. The upturned hull of the kayak appeared huge and ugly in the water, and I was worried why Fred hadn't surfaced. I held my breath and decided to take a look under the boat. Just then Fred appeared, coughing and spluttering.

"I got my bloody arse trapped in the seat!" he shouted, gasping for breath, with a rifle still strapped to his back. The very next second he started swimming for the bank in a very impressive front crawl reminiscent of Jonny Weissmuller's Tarzan in the movies. I'd never seen Fred swim as fast, which was the point I mentioned on the *Capetown Castle* when he claimed he was a very poor swimmer. He was out of the water and standing on dry land well ahead of me. It was amazing how the incentive of swimming in a crocodile lake can improve performance!

We lost our lunch, some spinners, and our new rods Van had given us, but we considered ourselves extremely lucky. We laughed and shook our heads, grateful that we'd not been passing the mud flats when I stupidly decided to stand up in the kayak. We were both surprised at how quickly it had flipped over, and I remarked to Fred about the bumping sensation and he stated he had felt it too. Luckily we could see our boat was drifting very slowly towards the end of the lake near the dam, followed by the paddles, so we returned to the car. The water bag was on my back, and I had biltong on my belt, so all was not lost. Fred opened the breach of the rifle and laid it down carefully in the sun to dry. We stripped naked and hung all our clothes on the branches of trees and bushes around us. Our cotton shirts and shorts dried very quickly, and less than an hour later we were grabbing at the kayak in the water and retrieving it with a long stick I'd ripped from a tree.

We re-launched and headed far down the lake past the mud flats. I looked longingly at the cool clear water, so once we'd passed the worst of the crocodile area, I prepared a spinner with one of our original old fishing rods and cast it over the side. I didn't expect to catch anything but to my surprise we did, and quite soon after I hauled in a beautiful fish, the biggest we'd yet caught, which flopped and flapped about in the kayak making every effort to escape. Fred despatched it with a sharp blow to the head and it flickered and twitched briefly before its life finally drained away. We were incredibly proud of our catch so we decided to land the kayak at the nearest point to Livingstone's village. We climbed out and secured the boat, then carried the fish as he had done, neatly wrapped in some large leaves, before setting off in search of Livingstone.

We followed a track which frequently seemed to vanish in front of us, but with new found confidence and some impressive bush craft we soon managed to find the village. We walked towards the huts to a surprised but tumultuous welcome, and Livingstone came up to us smiling broadly, shaking our hands in turn with his customary enthusiasm. I gave him the fish, which he initially refused but then accepted, with some profuse gratitude. I tried to explain that this may have been our last visit. I'm not sure he understood, but I suspect he did, because he suddenly looked quite serious and sat us down outside his hut, offering us more fruit juice and biltong. I then saw him talking to some others and glancing occasionally towards us, before disappearing inside, re-emerging moments later with some wooden objects in his arms. He handed us four of his beautiful animal carvings, which consisted of an elephant and antelope each. The wood had been carved glass-smooth and the legs of the antelope were incredibly thin and delicate. The elephants had white tusks and the antelope had antlers, fashioned from either ivory or animal bone. It didn't seem possible that these beautiful things could have been made from single pieces of solid wood with such rudimentary tools. Fred and I held the objects in our hands reverently and stared at them, drawing our fingers over the smooth wood in awe of the craftsmanship. Livingstone was quite insistent we take them and offered us a large animal skin bag we could use to carry them. I gently placed all four into the bottom and after more time spent alternately drinking juice and eating fresh biltong, we reluctantly stood up to leave. Many enthusiastic handshakes later, as though we'd never be able to leave, we started to make our way out of the village. I was very sad to leave, and I could tell that Fred was too. We knew it could have been our final visit. As it turned out it was, and I never saw Livingstone or his village again.

The conversation on the drive back to Broken Hill was subdued, but occasionally punctuated by some laughter about the capsizing of the kayak. I think we both secretly realised it would be the last time either of us would see Mulungushi Dam. We were driving west towards Broken Hill, towards the sunset, the deep yellow sky turning crimson, then an increasingly deep red, almost the colour of blood. The Black Watch were doing their rounds early when we arrived home just after dark. Their chanting sounded anomalous and slightly sinister, and the smell seemed far worse than before.

The following weekend I was invited to a '*braai*', a barbeque, at Van's house. It was Saturday afternoon and there was a fair breeze so I took a couple of my kites along with me. There was a wonderful atmosphere and Charlotte and Junior thoroughly enjoyed my kite flying lessons. Van's garden was of course huge, and the air was filled with the aroma of steak on the *braai,* the warm wind catching the smoke and sending it whirling around the garden. Charlotte and I were ordered to go upstairs to the piano and play for the guests, with the windows thrown open for all to hear. The music was received with loud applause from downstairs and in the garden, and between playing Charlotte skipped around the house and garden clearly in excellent spirits. I took some of the harvest from my garden to Van's, and later we ate some of my carrots and peas with the steak. The ranger, Mike, was at the *braai* and we laughed when I told him of our capsizing incident. I mentioned how quickly the kayak had turned over, as though pushed up from underneath, trying to find some alternative, palliative reason for the capsize other than my simply standing up. He suddenly looked quite serious at me, with a contemplative expression as though deep in thought.

"You know, it could have been a hippo…" he said finally, raising his eyebrows, "It could have been underneath the kayak," and I suspect he could sense my incredulity so he carried on: "They walk on the bottom, in deep water, and come up for air anywhere. If it was, and it sounds as though it could have been, then you were both very lucky, very lucky indeed. They can be nasty you know."

I tried to remember where I'd heard a warning about hippos before, and then I realised just how lucky Fred and I had been, yet again. Mike then looked up at the sky with a distant, almost melancholic expression on his face as though reading the gathering clouds.

"The rains will be here soon…" he said quite softly and to no-one in particular, then walked away towards the house. I looked up and was alarmed at just how much it had clouded over, with huge, dark blue cumulous gathering in force high above. I couldn't remember whether I noticed this phenomenon the previous year, but now it seemed so obvious. The clouds had gathered together slowly, taking their time, as though ganging up and conspiring against the clear blue with overwhelming force, building for weeks in preparation before bursting angrily over the parched earth. I followed Mike into the house to eat. Coffee and canasta followed the *braai,* and I returned to the bungalow later than ever.

Over the next few weeks I made frequent visits to Van's and gave Charlotte as many piano lessons as she could cope with in the upstairs room, which became known as the 'piano room' and even 'Charlotte and Dennis's room'.

On one such visit, one which actually became the last piano lesson, I tried to concentrate on the music but found it difficult when I realised that Charlotte was edging closer to me on the piano stool each time and to me she appeared prettier than ever. I dared to think that there may have been the beginning of some deep connection between us, some chemistry that was taking place with no apparent encouragement from either of us. I pushed this to the back of my mind and tried to dismiss it. I wanted her to play some notes of 'Clair de Lune' with me.

"You need to help with this, you need to play your part again," I said, taking hold of her fingers and placing them on the black notes as I continued: "like this, you see, all the way up the keys…" and I showed her again where I wanted the notes to be played, on the B flat and D flat keys. She remembered immediately and her fingers stroked the keys slowly and elegantly. I tried to play the music while Charlotte's fingers touched the keys in perfect time, and it sounded wonderful. She held my hand and laughed loudly and joyously with her mellifluous, infectious laughter, and played it several times. It had passed twilight and suddenly Charlotte jumped up and turned out the light, allowing the silvery white glow of the moon to fill our room again.

"Let's play it again, Dennis," she kept saying, "let's play 'Clair de Lune', again please," she repeated, and I touched the keys gently as I noticed tears forming in her huge brown eyes. I asked her what was wrong, to which she suddenly kissed me with a passionate and yet strangely distant kiss then stood up and ran crying from the room.

I followed her and could hear her running down the stairs. I had no idea what was wrong and when I reached the hallway Van saw me and called me into his study. I immediately thought I'd upset Charlotte somehow and felt ready for some questioning and perhaps some disapproving words, but I soon realised why Charlotte was so upset.

Van's study had the appearance of a small library; one wall was solid with bookshelves, and the room smelt of leather and stale cigar smoke. He sat on the edge of his huge desk with his arms folded and asked me how the piano lessons were going. He then became very serious and made me an offer that has stuck in my mind to this day:

"How would you like to join us at the mine, Dennis? You can come on board at the end of your contract, or else I'm sure

I can pull a few strings so you can start sooner, if you like?" and he handed me a large sealed envelope. "The terms and conditions are in here. It means a lot more money, and a renewed contract. Don't open it until you've decided what you want to do. But you are welcome to join us…"

I took hold of the envelope, utterly shocked and clueless as to what I should do. Van carried on: "It would mean you could join us in Natal. You would work with me, not here, but in Pietermaritzburg. You see, we are all moving down there as a family in a few weeks…" I wondered if this was the reason why Charlotte had been crying. I was stunned at this sudden offer, and my head filled with bizarre and confusing thoughts of Fred and our life together in the bungalow, and of returning to England. I felt as though I couldn't cope with this sudden change in plans, but I knew it was forcing me to make a decision sooner than I'd wanted to, but an inevitable decision nonetheless. If I'd been a drinking man there's no doubt I would have demanded a large scotch at that moment.

I knew that I had to let the railways know very soon whether I was staying or returning to England, and Van's timing was impeccable. He knew my situation, but had now made the decision even harder.

I walked across Broken Hill and returned to our bungalow. I was surprised to find Fred was still awake and sitting at the kitchen table. His eyes were bloodshot and he was pale, as though he'd had a recurrence of his malaria.

"Are you alright?" I asked him, "You don't look too good," and I made my way to the stove to boil some water for tea, placing the envelope on the table. It was oppressively hot that night, particularly in our bungalow, and Fred was sitting in his shorts, his naked bronze chest heaving and glistening in the pale white from the ceiling light.

"I think Alec's got the job in Salisbury. If he has, then they'll be leaving in a couple of weeks." And he looked at me, with a distant, vacant expression, as though pleading for reassurance.

"So you'll lose your canasta friends, eh?" I said, aware that I was probably not as sympathetic as I should have been.

"I'll never see them again, Dennis…" Fred replied, and suddenly I could see why he was upset. He'd formed a close relationship with both of them, and to lose them would be awful for him.

"Then it's decision time for both of us, Fred," I said, pointing to the envelope, "I've been offered a renewed contract and a change of posting, to go with Van and his family, and I've no idea what to do…" I said, and I saw Fred repeatedly rubbing his forehead with both hands. I noticed his hands were shaking, trembling almost.

He looked up at me with desperation in his eyes: "Dennis, tell me, how did we get into this mess?"

RAIN

I didn't sleep well at all that night; my mind was racing with thoughts of staying in Africa, or returning to England. I dreamt of Charlotte, Van's house, the dam, Fred, indeed everything important to me about Africa. I kept waking up in fits of anxiety, lathered in sweat, naked as a baby under my mosquito net. Fred's door was open and I could hear him moving about in his room, as restless as I was. Dawn finally broke revealing a cloudy and overcast day. A wind had developed which whipped around our bungalow, rattling and tugging at the corrugated iron roof, as though generated by our own restless night and turbulent thoughts. I had a simple choice and was to mark the envelope Van had given me with 'Africa' or 'England' and deliver it to him once I'd made my decision. My best friend and confidant was also in turmoil so I had no-one to talk it over with. I needed advice, someone who would help make the decision for me.

All day my thoughts were on Van and his family, but more particularly on Charlotte. We'd grown very close and I could see this would most likely develop further if I stayed. But I was due to go home to England and Sheffield in order to resume my life there. Africa meant promotion, more money, and continued adventure. I had to make one of the hardest, most important and far-reaching decisions of my entire life.

I finished work just after three o'clock as usual and made my way home to our bungalow. I was due to start a final 'sit' in a large bungalow some distance away, not far from 'crap alley', so I washed and changed and picked up the key to the house from the kitchen drawer. We were usually given two keys for each 'sit'. I didn't notice the other one was missing.

I discovered that Fred was out, and had left a rather erratic and untidy handwritten note on the kitchen table: *Going out – gone for a while – see you much later – Fred*. I guessed he'd gone to Alec and Diana's so he would probably be home very late, as it suggested in the note. I locked the bungalow and left. I remember I worked a pretty standard shift at the club and then walked briskly to Van's. The atmosphere at Van's house that night was unlike anything I'd ever known before. Outside the night air was sticky and oppressive, typical of the days just before the rains, and inside it was also very subdued and quiet. Van appeared strangely distant and preoccupied, wandering in and out of his study, carrying paperwork around and shuffling it about on his desk. Charlotte broke out in tears quite spontaneously, and I found it incredibly uncomfortable. We ate a meal as usual but it was an unhappy and difficult occasion. I was still undecided as to what I should do, but I began to realise, as though waking up from a lengthy but beautiful dream, that I would probably return to England. Maybe Van could sense this. I left very early for the first time, and began to walk through the streets of Broken Hill to my 'sit'. Conflicting ideas and images were raging around inside my head.

Dark clouds had gathered around us and without warning as I walked, tortured and distracted by my own thoughts, the whole of Broken Hill suddenly lit up as bright as midday when a brilliant blue-white lightning flash filled the night sky. An increasingly brutal wind took hold of the trees, bending them over, scattering leaves and branches across roads and pathways. The thunder that followed exploded all around me with such intensity I felt the earth shudder under my feet. There was no-one else around, and I felt as though this entire phenomenon was directed specifically at me, alone. Rain then fell heavily in a blanket of huge drops, soaking my clothing in an instant. The air filled with the rare and fabulous odour of rain falling on long dry earth, and so I started to run, slowly at first, but then very gradually quickening my pace. I could feel my hair was heavy and wet, and rainwater was pouring down my face into my eyes and onto my lips. I remember thinking for an instant how good it tasted, so cool and refreshing. I reached the very grand bungalow where I was to stay the night and leapt up three front steps onto the veranda in one stride, and started fumbling in the pockets of my wet shorts for the key. I pushed it into the lock but to my surprise I could see there was a key on the inside already, so I couldn't unlock the door.

I didn't understand this, and peered through the glass in the front door. The house was completely dark. More lightning and thunder followed, and I stood on the veranda listening at the door. There was no sound from inside so I walked around the veranda and peered in the windows. The interior rooms were in darkness but were lit beautifully and briefly by the instantaneous flashes of lightning, and I could see it was exactly as it should have been. I moved to the left and over to one of the bedrooms and leaned close to the steel-framed glass to see inside.

To my astonishment I saw there was movement at the far side against the wall, on the bed. As I stared between lightning flashes I couldn't comprehend the fact that this movement was clearly from more than one person, and for an instant I felt as though I recognised at least one of them. There was more than one pair of arms, more than two legs, more than one human being lying there on that bed. This couldn't be possible! I immediately thought someone, some stranger, had managed to get inside the house and was in there now, with another person. Did I really suspect, deep down, just who it might have been? I think I probably did, but I didn't want to admit it to myself. I had to get inside and see who it was, to confirm exactly who it was, to see what they were doing and what was happening.

I kicked loudly at the front door several times with my right foot, and I could see the wood beginning to splinter and crack. But then it was opened, by Fred, wearing a pair of shorts that were unfastened, back to front, and obviously put on in a hurry. Diana appeared in the hallway behind him and was dressing quickly, mumbling to herself over and over. I turned on the light and looked at them both. Without thinking, and in a blind fit of jealous rage, I threw a punch at Fred with my right clenched fist which contacted with his nose and sent him reeling backwards. He landed heavily and after a brief pause he stood up and ran towards me. Fred collided with me and I fell backwards and we rolled on the floor each trying to get a punch on the other. Neither of us were fighters of any sort and it probably looked very messy, but there was real fury on my part. My very best friend in the entire world – my *only* friend in the entire world – had betrayed me for someone else – and with Diana! How could this happen? I couldn't believe it! What had happened to all the trust built up between us, after all we'd been through, all our adventures and promises to each other?

I shouted at Fred: "You rotten lousy bastard, Fred, you're a first class cad and a traitor!" just as I started sobbing and trying to get another punch on him.

I heard Fred shout back at me: "Dennis, it's not what you think, honestly…" as we pushed and punched one another.

Then I heard Diana's voice, pleading: "Dennis, please, Fred, please stop!" just as Fred released his grip on my shoulders and staggered to his feet, moving away from me. I lay on the floor on my back and looked up. Fred and Diana were standing in the doorway to the bedroom in a close embrace. I stood up, fully intent upon carrying on, but then Diana looked at me with tears flooding down her face: "Don't tell Alec, please…" and went on: "he'll be back from Salisbury later tonight, he doesn't need to know, please!" and she looked at me; pleading with me.

I had no idea what to say, and heard myself asking: "What the hell do you think you're both doing?" as I rose to my feet, and I know it probably sounded pathetic, but I reminded Fred that we had sworn that day by the dam that neither of us would ever become tangled up in any sordid, extra-marital affairs.

"Dennis, this is our last night, Diana and Alec leave for Salisbury in a few days, this is it, the end…" Fred tried in vain to take hold of my right hand in his, but I stepped away, and stood blankly staring at him, then at Diana, conscious of more tears beginning to gather uncontrollably in my own eyes. In a blind rage I lunged at him and hit him again, as punishment for his hypocrisy, after everything we'd said on our expeditions and had confided in each other. Fred fought back and we fell out the front door onto the veranda. We rolled down the steps onto the grass in the front garden. Fred shouted: "You've been getting close to Charlotte, you've told me so yourself, we're all human beings Dennis," as he suddenly became more aggressive.

"She's not married though; she doesn't have a husband does she?" I replied, shocked when I saw Fred's face was bleeding, his nose and lips broken open from where I'd hit him. His expression was of deep anger and surprise, and I hated myself for what I was doing, but I couldn't control my rage. In the lightning flashes I could see spots of blood mixed with rainwater on our clothing and smeared across Fred's face and down onto his chest. We continued rolling around alternately trying to hit and then restrain one another, and I became aware that I was gradually getting the upper hand. Eventually, after what seemed hours but was probably only a few minutes, Fred collapsed, at the verge near 'crap alley', utterly exhausted. He lay motionless on the wet ground at my feet, and Diana ran up to me. I looked at her and shouted: "Here's your darling Fred. Whatever were you thinking about? You're as guilty as he is. Just do what you want with him!" and I staggered back towards the house, breathless and shaking, leaving them both. Up the steps onto the veranda I saw untidy smears of blood spread across the wooden floor where we'd been rolling around, and they continued back into the hallway. The rain poured from the corrugated roof of the house, flashes of lightning emphasised the blood-soaked floor and the thunder occasionally pounded the atmosphere like exploding artillery shells. The house suddenly seemed part of some bloody gothic horror or somewhere on the front line in a combat zone.

I found a bed and threw myself on it. I felt incredibly alone. I thought of what I'd just done to Fred and I was filled with remorse and guilt. I cried like I'd never cried before. My thoughts then turned to Charlotte, who was by then seventeen, and whether we had any future together. It was all here, ready and waiting. Suddenly, Fred and Diana's affair made me realise nothing was impossible. I allowed myself some wild, outrageous thoughts. Yes, I could stay, I could live in Africa forever, with Charlotte, and we *could* do it! Look what Fred had done! Who would have thought?

I heard the rain and wind around the house as I lay on the bed. My hand throbbed where I'd hit Fred, and gradually a dark wave of cool common sense swept over me. It was impossible, I realised, and it had all been just a silly fantasy. I was caught up in the African heat, as Fred and Diana had been, as everyone seemed to be eventually. Rational sensibilities seemed to ebb away from you the longer you stayed there, away from the cold harsh realities of life in England. I shut my eyes and within seconds I was unconscious.

DIANA

When I woke up the rain had stopped. The sun was streaming in the windows and for a moment I wondered where I was. My hands and face hurt like hell. Some of my ribs were very painful. Then I remembered what had happened, and I felt sick. I rolled off the bed and stood up. I don't know why but I found a cloth and washed the blood from the wooden floor. It had dried and was difficult to remove. I stepped out the front door and locked the house behind me. I looked across to where I last saw Fred near 'crap alley' but he was gone. I wandered vacantly back towards our bungalow. Fred hadn't come home. I assumed that he'd stayed at Diana's but I then realised Alec had been due home. I wondered where he was, and where he'd slept the night. I managed to gather myself sufficiently to change and tidy myself up a bit. I looked in the mirror but didn't recognise myself. The man staring back at me was suddenly much older and bruised. This was what anguish, betrayal and regret looked like. I was empty and exhausted, and was aware I was probably behaving like an automaton, but I managed to drag myself to work. No-one spoke to me even though I must have appeared to have been behaving in an unusually quiet manner, the marks on my face testament to something which I clearly did not wish to discuss. I looked for Fred at work, but he wasn't there. Alec and Diana were not in work either. Where were the three of them?

I arrived home at the bungalow just after three-thirty that afternoon to be greeted by Bert, Fred's 'boy'. He was shouting and was very agitated about something. I tried unsuccessfully to calm him down and I asked him what was wrong. He said: "*Bwana* Fred, *bwana* Fred, medic, medic!" and he continued shouting, and pointing towards the mine. Something very serious had clearly happened to Fred overnight. I walked briskly, almost at a running pace towards the mine hospital. I mentioned

190

Fred's name at the admissions desk and was immediately sent towards the intensive care department. Probably with desperation written all across my face I blundered from one member of staff to another trying to find him.

"What's happened to Mr Leach?" I begged one of the nurses outside the intensive care unit.

"Snake bite," she replied succinctly, eyebrows raised, "we got to him just in time too, but as it is he's in a coma…"

"Will he be alright?" I asked pleadingly

"Should be, now, but he was lucky," she replied,

"Do you know what happened?" I asked, trying to look the nurse in the eyes.

"He was found collapsed in the road this morning, and someone brought him here, that's all I know."

I was refused access to him, so I sat on a chair in the corridor, not really knowing what I should do. I discovered that someone had found Fred lying in the undergrowth near 'crap alley' where I'd last seen him, and he was probably bitten by the snake then, while he lay there unconscious. I wondered whether it had been Diana who had gone for help, but no-one seemed able to tell me. I sat for hours in the hospital, unable to make sense of how and why my wonderful time in Africa was rapidly descending into nightmare. Eventually I realised I'd sat there all afternoon, as I could see the light was fading quickly outside. The Rhodesian twilight fell with its usual brevity, like a huge blanket thrown across the sky, so I pulled myself up and started to walk home.

I couldn't face working in the club; I didn't feel like doing anything at all. I made myself a coffee and sat at my kitchen table. I put on the light and the bungalow was screaming emptiness at me. Fred's bedroom door was open, and I wondered how many times Diana had been there when I was out, probably at Van's house. I stared down at my coffee with my head resting heavily in my hands, and a wave of exhaustion swept over me. I was beginning to fall asleep, sitting there at the table, when there was a series of loud and frantic bangs on the front door.

"Hubbard! Mr Hubbard! Are you in there?" A man's gruff Afrikaner voice was repeatedly shouting my name, the words echoing throughout the bungalow. I walked over to the door, suddenly worried what I would find. I opened it and there were two Afrikaner policemen from the station down the road.

"You know Alec and Diana Richardson, is that right?" one of them demanded, and I could see both had Webley pistols in holsters, and they were each carrying a rifle on their right shoulder.

"Yes, I do, why?"

"They're both missing," and seeing my vacant look then said, in a more conciliatory tone: "can you help us find them?" to which I nodded, but really I had no idea where they might be, or even if they were still in Broken Hill.

I walked with the two officers to Alec and Diana's house, but it was clear as we arrived they were not there. The front door was open, and some lights were on, but the house was empty. I noticed Alec's rifle was missing. I didn't think to tell anyone. The two policemen spoke briefly to one another in Afrikaans, and then we were joined by another who mentioned there had been a report of something unusual at the pool area, which was supposedly out of bounds to everyone at night. I heard the Afrikaans word '*swembad*' so I walked with the three policemen towards the pool. There was no conversation, and the three men had quiet, serious expressions on their faces. I followed but was unsure what help I was providing in the effort.

I suppose I knew right from the start exactly who it was, standing at the top of the steps up to the diving board. It was clearly a woman, as the outline of her dress was visible, as was her long hair over her shoulders. The three policemen paused, allowing me to pass them, to be the first to get close to this person. I shouted but there was no response. It was twilight, almost dark, and there were still some people in the pool, at the far end, chatting closely together. Others were standing around the edge of the pool and the usual light-hearted relaxed pool-side atmosphere quickly changed. I can see my feet now,

192

climbing those metal steps, blissfully unaware as I was at the time. I wasn't to know the level of pain and desperation in Diana's mind. I was just there to ask her what she was doing, and to bring her down the steps safely, and maybe to take her for a cup of coffee, to visit Fred, and for everything to be alright. I couldn't have known what she was contemplating. I reached the top step and she turned to face me, hanging onto the steel rail.

She looked directly at me: "Alec didn't get the job, Dennis. You know what that means. I can't live here anymore, I just can't..." Then I realised she was trembling, and sobbing hysterically. The top of the diving board was probably only fifteen feet above ground, but it was almost as high as a house, and Diana was leaning against the railings over the side, and not over the water.

I suddenly had a bleak vision of what might happen, what could happen, so I shouted, pleadingly: "Diana, come here, please..." and I held out an arm, but I could see she wasn't listening. She then said something which at the time I didn't understand:

"I'm not bothered about Fred..." and then: "I told him so. I just want Alec and my baby..." and she calmly moved closer to the end of the railing. I was confused, but then she said: "Alec's taken his gun. He's looking for Fred." She looked at me, blankly, with an expression in her face that I'll never forget, and then said to me very calmly: "Goodbye Dennis!" while staring straight into my eyes. I tried to grab hold of her but she leaned over the side above the concrete and simply released her grip. For a split second she stood unsupported, motionless in space and completely free, before she started to lean over, slowly at first, but then accelerating, rolling over, tall and straight, like a felled tree. She dropped silently through the early evening air, through the empty space between the diving board and the ground, rushing headlong in an irreversible fateful dive onto the solid concrete below.

I know there was an awful noise when Diana made contact with the poolside, because I was told this by others present.

But I didn't hear it. I was being sick, right there on the top of the diving board steps. I heard women near the pool screaming and men's voices shouting commands and swearing in both English and Afrikaans. I started shaking violently with severe shock. I was sick again and suddenly I found myself being grabbed tightly and irresistibly from both sides and virtually dragged back down the steps. I was pulled away from the poolside but in the melee I know I heard the Afrikaans words: '*Sy is dood*': 'She's dead'.

CHARLOTTE AND ALEC

My connection to Van was well known so I was taken there. The house was in uproar. Charlotte was usually the first to greet me but was nowhere to be seen. Goldie was sobbing hysterically and Van approached me and said: "Charlotte's in the hospital, she's taken some of Goldie's sleeping tablets, and she's in a bad way…" I couldn't believe what I was hearing; this was all a nightmare, surely?

"Dennis, you'd better come and see this," Van instructed me to follow him up the stairs to Charlotte's bedroom, the room so clearly marked with 'NO ENTRY' and 'PRIVATE' on the door. It seems the servants had been inside to clean, but Charlotte had not allowed anyone else in there for months. Van opened the door and ushered me inside. I looked around me, shocked and surprised. Every wall had photographs of me stuck across it, in various sizes, dozens of them, all taken by her brother Junior and developed at home. There were idiot smiling faces of me in my cricket whites, football kit, in the garden, by the pool, at their house, from all over. I knew Junior had been pointing his camera in my direction but half the time I didn't realise he was using film, and even then I had no idea what was going to happen to all the photographs. I felt incredibly foolish and embarrassed, to add further to the utter devastation that I already felt from earlier.

My first instinct was to turn to Van, shaking my head and with a deep sigh I simply said to him: "I'm sorry, I had no idea…"

Van just looked at me, forcing a smile, then in reply said: "Dennis, it's not your fault," before leading me back down the stairs. He then suggested we visit the hospital and I agreed. Fred was still there and now Charlotte was also a patient. I kept making profuse apologies to him about Charlotte, for probably leading her on and being the subject of her infatuation, but he accepted my apologies, as he knew it was sincere. I remember passing near our bungalow in Van's car and seeing my 'boy', John, sitting outside as though waiting for me. I asked Van to make a detour so I could speak to him. We pulled up and as soon as he saw me John started shouting frantically:

"*Bwana* Alec gone, *bwana. Bwana* Alec gone with gun!"

I could hear Van reply, almost under his breath: "Bloody hell!" and he spoke to John in a mixture of Shona and Afrikaans, extracting some more information.

"It seems Alec called round to see you not long ago. He's pissed out of his mind, he's found out about Diana, and he's gone on the rampage with his rifle!" and I saw Van looked distraught. I then suddenly remembered some of Diana's last words about Alec and his gun and I told Van what she'd said. How could this get any worse? Suddenly everything took on a greater urgency.

"What are you going to do?" I asked him, rather lamely, just as we climbed back into the car.

"We'll have to sort this out!" he said, not knowing who he meant by 'we'. "He'll probably go to the mine hospital, he knows Fred's there," and he insisted that whatever happened I was to stay in the car and not get involved.

We drove at high speed around Broken Hill and pulled up sharply outside the hospital. Van jumped out the car immediately, instructing me again to stay where I was. He was joined by two mine security guards who ran up towards the car carrying automatic rifles. They looked anxious and were lathered in sweat, their faces glistening in the bright glow from the car headlights. I tried to hear their conversation, but it was quick, in short bursts and in Afrikaans, and they were constantly turning their heads and pointing towards the hospital.

I opened the car door slowly and eased myself silently out the car while Van and the two guards were having an increasingly heated discussion. Several police officers arrived on foot and then I heard one of them shout: "*Daar!*" and pointed to the side of the building. A dark figure was stooped over, lurking around peering in the windows, one after the other. This anonymous person was obviously very unsteady on his feet, as he rolled and swayed as he walked, fast and then slow, as though having to keep checking himself. He was carrying something long and metallic in his arms in front of him, which occasionally caught a glint of light like shiny polished steel. It was Alec with his rifle.

Against the background a of plain brick wall Alec was caught in several torchlights and for a moment stood perfectly still, frozen in the light, startled like a rabbit in a road. He held his rifle in his right hand and lifted his left arm to shield his face.

"Put it down, man!" shouted one of the policemen, then: "Drop the rifle!" and for a hopeful few seconds I thought Alec would comply. He took hold of his gun with both hands and seemed to lower it so the barrel was pointing towards the ground. He'd drop it to the ground and then it would all be over. It would be the end of the nightmare, with Alec coming to his senses and giving up.

One of the mine security guards shouted something inaudible from where I was standing next to the car, and then I saw Alec lift up his rifle in response and aim it directly at him. It was the two mine security guards who fired first. I don't know how many times they fired at Alec, but he didn't stand a chance. The rifles cracked loudly several times in the night air and bullets ripped into him one after the other, tearing his clothing and sending him flying backwards as though hit by an express train. I watched in open-mouthed horror as he fell to the ground. I couldn't comprehend what I was seeing.

Suddenly my legs gave way underneath me and I found myself on my knees next to the car. I was shaking and screaming, banging my fists into the dirt until my knuckles hurt. There was a flurry of activity around Alec and he was covered in a blanket, rolled up, and carried away. One of the mine security guards came directly over to me and I remember exactly what he said to me:

"You know nothing about this incident man, right?" and I nodded, blubbering snot and tears streaming down my face.

Van had disappeared and I was left alone on the grass. The rain had stopped as quickly as it had started and now a bright full moon appeared between lengthening breaks in the dark clouds. The African moon, like no other, stared down at me as though in pity, tormenting me, mocking me. I staggered back towards my bungalow.

Close to our bungalow my neighbours Janet and Colin appeared and spoke to me. I could hardly hear what they were saying but they ushered me into their house, insisting I had a stiff drink. They seemed to know what had happened and kept repeating how terrible it all was, as though I didn't already know. I sat in a complete daze at their kitchen table, empty and totally numb. I refused the drink and I heard them talking about me, a few feet away, and then they turned and started talking directly at me. I wasn't listening, I was there, in the room, with them, but then I wasn't. I was outside the hospital and then I was at the poolside. I just wanted to sleep. I was becoming overwhelmed by a powerful desire to leave it all, to get away somehow, to escape.

Whatever next could happen to me? My entire world was collapsing around me, and there was nothing I could do about it. It was then that I was offered a way out. I was given a handful of enormous sleeping tablets by Janet and instructed to take half a tablet and then another half if I found that wasn't enough.

I was helped into my own bedroom and was lowered onto my bed. Finally I was left alone. Every time I closed my eyes I saw Diana falling from the diving board, and Alec collapsing in a bloodied heap outside the hospital. I wanted to get away from all this. It all hurt far too much for me to cope with. I didn't know what I wanted any more, or even who I was. I picked up the sleeping tablets I'd been given and swallowed them all down together at once in a glass of water.

THE END

I was walking in bright sunlight towards Van's house; the light was so bright that I had to shield my eyes. I was happy and content, my heart was racing, and I was excited at the prospect of seeing them all again. Charlotte answered the door wearing her prettiest thin cotton dress, and she greeted me with a warm smile and her usual sweetness.

"Hello Dennis," and she took my hand and kissed me, saying: "I've been waiting for you all my life," as she pulled me through the house, which was white and very bright, but there was thick dust on the floor, and everywhere I looked. The house smelt strangely musty and unclean, as though it had been abandoned and locked up for months. Charlotte drifted across the floor like an angel, and she looked incredibly happy and beautiful. I looked around me but I saw that there was no-one else in the house.

"Where is everyone?" I asked her, as I could see each room was quiet and empty.

"They've all gone. We're all alone now," she replied, mischievously,

"Gone? Gone where?" I said, confused,

"Just gone," she said, as she pulled my hand and led me up the stairs to the piano room. Inside, the piano was lit purely by a thick, concentrated shaft of moonlight from the window and it shimmered very eerily in a silvery white glow.

"No need to put the light on," Charlotte said, "just look up at the man in the moon, I can see him smiling at us Dennis, he's happy!" and we sat side by side on the piano stool. I looked at my hands in front of me and they were shaking violently. I couldn't stop them shaking, they were beyond my control, as if they were someone else's, but they were *my* hands. The piano keys were shining and sparkling like diamonds in bright sunlight, and Charlotte spoke to me:

"Play the moon Dennis, please, play the moon," and despite my trembling hands I started to play 'Clare de Lune' as we usually did, and she played the length of the keyboard as I'd taught her, playing the black notes, and it sounded incredibly beautiful. She kissed me again and again as she moved her hands up and down the keyboard in perfect time, then suddenly she stood up and walked across the room. She stopped in a corner by the window and placed a record on a turntable, and turned up the volume very high. It crackled into life as the needle rode the vinyl surface, and music started to completely fill the room, smothering us utterly and igniting the flames between us. It was 'Clare de Lune', and it echoed all around us, as though the whole orchestra was in there with us.

Charlotte walked back over to the piano and unfastened the top button of her blouse. She invited me to carry on releasing more of the buttons by taking my hand, and I complied. I removed my own shirt and my shorts until we were both standing there in the moonlight, completely naked. Charlotte moved over to a sofa near the piano, a brilliant white sofa I'd never seen before, and lay across it, waiting for me. I moved over to her.

"Charlotte, you look like an angel…" I whispered, and she gripped my hand tightly. Suddenly Charlotte started shivering uncontrollably and she held my hand tighter than ever.

She shouted: "Dennis! Dennis!" and I watched as she began to fade and started to disappear as though falling away from me. I reached for her but she fell too quickly and I couldn't catch her. I tried desperately to grab her but in a few seconds she faded away completely and was gone.

I opened my eyes with a start. I was on my back, staring up at a brilliant white ceiling. A strange woman, a nurse, was gripping my right hand very hard, squeezing it intermittently.

"Mr Hubbard, Dennis, wake up. I think you've been having a nightmare," and I looked around, unable to work out where I was.

"You're in the mine hospital. We had to break in. You'd

200

not been seen all day. We think you'd been unconscious for fourteen hours."

I looked around me, trying to gather my thoughts. I tried to remember what had happened. Then Van appeared. I was very confused and couldn't concentrate. My mind was unclear as though my head had been filled with cotton wool. Everything seemed unreal. I couldn't understand what was happening, and where reality began and my dreams ended. I remember I asked Van about Charlotte.

"She's here, but she's alright. She'll be fine. She took the news very badly that you were going back to England. I presume that's what you're doing?"

I didn't answer the question, but replied with another: "Can I see her, please?" To which Van replied: "I don't think that would be a good idea. She's accepted what's happening. It might just upset her."

I reached for my wallet and took out the photograph of Esther I'd carried with me since leaving England two years before. Van took it from me and stared at it.

"I do believe hidden in that photograph is the answer to it all, Dennis, for you at least. Esther looks a lovely girl. No wonder England beckons." I nodded in agreement, and sighed. Van smiled and handed the photograph back to me. He stood by my bed for a few moments, looking at me.

"Goodbye Dennis. My family will always remember you with great affection, you crazy Englander," and he turned and walked out the door. I couldn't believe that was to be the last time I'd see him.

I was considering getting out of bed to follow him when just at that moment Charlotte walked in, looking as lovely as ever. She came over to the bed and picked up the photograph. She looked at it for what seemed several minutes.

"I'm going to say goodbye, but can I leave knowing that we are parting when we still love each other in our own special way?"

"Of course, Charlotte," I replied. She kissed me on the lips, turned, and in a moment she was gone. There were no tears from either of us.

I slept for the rest of the day and was discharged in the afternoon. In the few days after these horrific incidents I felt utterly unsociable and lived a detached, reclusive existence. I was due to leave so I was no longer working. I visited Fred in hospital, but stayed away from Van and his family, until the end of that week, when I decided to visit their house. I thought I perhaps ought to formally hand him his envelope, which I'd clearly marked 'ENGLAND' on both sides. I could vaguely remember seeing Van and Charlotte visiting my bedside in the hospital, but I wanted to say goodbye to them properly.

Strangely I found the house secure and no-one answered the door. I walked to the mine reception desk and asked to see Van. The pretty female receptionist looked at me with a puzzled expression: "I'm sorry but Mr Van der Merwe and his family moved to Pietermaritzburg yesterday. Can I send them a message?" and she looked at me, smiling in a very forced, insincere manner from behind her spotlessly clean and tidy desk.

"No, no, it doesn't matter…" I replied, hearing my own voice and thinking how weak it sounded, feeling as though it had been spoken by someone else. I remember I left the envelope on the desk, slightly in a daze, and I don't even know whether she noticed it or not. I returned to the bungalow walking alone through Broken Hill, feeling desperately, utterly sad.

Fred was now out of hospital and living back at home. He seemed weaker, and shuffled his feet around the bungalow like an old man in his slippers. We both spent the rest of the day packing. I had all four carved animals from Livingstone in the animal skin bag, and Fred told me to take them all with me, as he'd catch up with me later.

The next night we walked to the station together, as my train was due to leave for the Cape at ten forty-five. Fred couldn't board the train with me as he told me had to call in at Ndola for something before heading south again. His train north was due at any moment, and then he said he would be joining me in Cape Town for the boat home. I had no reason to doubt him. Suddenly he broke down in tears and took hold of my hand.

"Dennis I'm truly sorry." He collapsed onto his knees in front of me. "Please forgive me, please, before we part, please..." I hauled him up to his feet and we hugged one another closely, so tight I could hardly breathe. We were both crying by this time, and then he said: "I'm guilty of murder; I know I am, but I want to remember us as we were, please tell me you forgive me, please..." I took hold of his hand and shook it, trying to force a smile between the tears.

"Of course, Fred, it's there for the taking. I want to remember us as we were, at the dam, with the animals, Livingstone, the kayak, everything. I'll never forget it, any of it..." and just at that moment my train was ready to leave. I looked into the darkness down the line, south, and wondered what lay ahead, just as I had when I'd looked up the line north, two years before.

I climbed aboard and opened a window. I waved at Fred, now a forlorn looking, solitary figure in silhouette standing on the platform. He didn't wave back. This was not my Fred, not the one I'd shared all our adventures with. There was a distance in his eyes, and his spirit was dull and saddened. I hated leaving him there at the station, but he insisted he would be following on. It wasn't until my train had pulled away that I realised there were no trains to Ndola that night.

I sat alone with my thoughts on that desperate and awful five day train journey back to Cape Town. The noisy, malodourous train clattered and banged its way relentlessly south, further away from all I knew. I remembered how naïve and innocent I'd been on the outward journey, and felt much of me had been left there in Broken Hill, parts of my soul that would remain there forever. I vowed to myself right there and then that I would never reveal to anyone the terrible details of my last days in Africa.

The journey was irksome and tedious, and I was frequently talked at by other passengers and I nodded politely in reply where I thought it appropriate. But my mind was elsewhere, thinking of Alec and Diana, wondering if I could have done more to help, torturing myself with feelings of acute regret and remorse. The vast African landscape and the wild animals passed me by as I sat staring out the window, wallowing in my own self-pity, the oppressive heat inside the train hardly bothering me.

In Cape Town I waited for Fred all day at the docks before boarding the boat. Fred never arrived.

I had my own cabin again, this time on *The Stirling Castle* for the two week voyage to Southampton. It was Saturday November 29th 1952.

My cabin was clean and bright, but very small. I was grateful for a bath after the return train journey, and lay on my bed staring at the one and only porthole in my cabin. I felt incredibly alone. Where had everyone and everything gone?

We'd been at sea for several hours when a member of the crew knocked on the door. He confirmed my name, then handed me a letter. My heart leapt when I could see it was Fred's handwriting. I opened it and began to tremble as I started reading a short note:

Dennis, don't blame yourself, or anyone for what's happened. It's all finished. Diana's gone, Alec's gone, now you and Charlotte. I only just found out that my mother died several months ago. Now I have nothing. By the time you read this I'll be gone too. You always said I couldn't hit a barn door, but not this time. I'm going to the dam, Dennis, our dam. I did tell you I'd rather die there than anywhere else. Please try not to think too badly of me, goodbye Dennis. Fred.

I sat on my bed and felt sick. I was gasping for air and felt as though I would pass out. I was desperate to inform someone of the letter, but it was already almost a week old. If Fred had wanted to do this then it had probably already been done. I read the letter several times. I suddenly felt as though the cabin walls would swallow me up and I had to get out. I staggered out of my stuffy little room and wandered towards the stern of the ship, dragging myself along, pulling at the hand rails, my legs weak and unsteady.

At the back of the ship the sea was being thrashed around by the propellers in a wide and turbulent wake. I stood alone, leaning on the rail, tears streaming down my face, my head feeling as though it was about to burst. I heard 'Clair de Lune' in my head and Charlotte laughing, then I looked down as I let go of Fred's letter and watched it gently flutter and drift like an autumn leaf onto the surface of the water. I wanted to follow it. I wanted to jump. I thought of Esther, and at that moment the prospect of seeing her again was probably the only thing that stopped me climbing over the rail.

"Life must go on, you know," a man's calming voice suddenly said to me from behind. I turned my head and saw it was a man I'd vaguely noticed had been on the same train, and had boarded the boat at the same time. He hauled me back down to earth with his gentle, mellifluous voice, coaxing me into life again, an inch at a time, until we both sat on the crisp, clean boards of the deck, leaning with our backs to the rail.

I'm afraid I unloaded all my problems onto his listening ears, and we then became friends for the entire two week voyage. His name was Martin, and his contract with the railways had also just expired.

As the days passed on *The Stirling Castle* I began to revive. We stopped briefly in Madeira where I bought fresh nuts to take home to Sheffield. I had long talks with Martin on the voyage home. To my astonishment I discovered that he had similar experiences of tragedy and romance too, during the time he had spent living in the greatest continent on earth: Africa.

EPILOGUE

As *The Stirling Castle* forced its way across the Bay of Biscay and entered the English Channel, I could hear the BBC on the radio, with Alvar Lidell reading the news. I was almost home. The weather was dreadful and it was much colder than anything I'd experienced in the previous two years. The boat pitched and rolled in a heavy swell, and salty sea spray filled the air, with anything out on deck becoming instantly soaked. Southampton was desperately dismal and grey, but I was actually very excited about being back on English soil once again. Africa filled my thoughts constantly, though I was learning to forget it, forcing myself to push it all to the back of my mind.

A particularly annoying fellow passenger was searched and his case was found to contain hundreds of contraband cigarettes. Martin and I smiled a little at his misfortune. Later, when we pulled into Waterloo, the same man revealed a bag of sweets which were not sweets at all but more than a dozen precious gemstones. He laughed and stepped off the train calling back to us: "Good day gentlemen!" before he disappeared into the dark and anonymous London streets.

My fiancée, Esther, met me at Sheffield's Victoria station. It was wonderful to see her again. Other than in a few scribbled letters home, no-one really knew of the tragic events in Africa, and that was how it remained until I forced myself to recall them for this book. Who would have believed me even if I'd told them?

My dad, Alf, greeted me at home with: "Weer's tha bin?" To which I replied: "Africa," as though the previous two years hadn't existed.

Esther and I were married a few months later on January 31st 1953, and we bought a small house in King's Lynn, Norfolk, with the money I'd brought back from Africa. We were then subjected to the Great Flood, during which the majority of my notes, photographs and documents from Africa were sadly lost. This book contains the best of those that survived.

I tried to follow events in Rhodesia over the years. Roy Welensky became Prime Minister of a new state called the Federation of Rhodesia and Nyasaland in 1956. He was later knighted, and eventually left Africa in 1980, and died in Dorset, England.

Rhodesia is of course now known as Zimbabwe and Broken Hill is called Kabwe, and is in fact now in Zambia. The mine caused so much pollution that the whole area around it today is classed as a poisonous area.

I've had no contact from anyone I knew in Africa. Charlotte was sixteen in 1950. To this day I've no idea what happened to her and her family, or to my other great friend, Fred Leach...

ACKNOWLEDGEMENTS

My sincere gratitude and admiration goes to Jonathan for making sense of my scribbled notes and few surviving pieces of memorabilia from my time in Africa. All those phone calls! This book would not have been possible without his support and encouragement. As you said, Jonathan, the late Dirk Bogarde was once told to '*Force Memory!*' which is precisely what I did! I'm sorry about all the tears, but I was true to the vow I made to myself all those years ago: this has been the first time I've ever told this story to anyone.

Thank you to my wife Esther, who has been by my side for these last sixty years. We have grandchildren and great-grandchildren, who will now be able to read of my exploits in Africa, when I wrestled with the crocodile on Mulungushi Lake! I know you may not believe some or all of it, but I can assure you it really did happen, exactly as it's been described.

Profuse thanks also go to Jeremy Thompson and his team at Matador. Finally, thanks also to the brilliant poet Charlotte Ballard for the use of her lovely poem, 'The Truth'.